My Lord
My Rock
My Life

W. Douglas Evans

Copyright© 1993 ECC Publications

All rights reserved. No part of this publication may be reproduced or transmitted in any form or by any means, electronic or mechanical, including photocopying, recording or informations storage and retrieval system, without permission in writing from the publisher.

ISBN 0-9521628-0-6
My Lord, My Rock, My Life (pbk)

This book is dedicated to all the people who have made it possible. It is the prayer of the author and everyone involved, that those who read it may experience for themselves the love of the Lord Jesus Christ. Luke 6 v. 48.

ECC Publications, 91 Main Road, Nether Kellet, Carnforth, Lancs LA6 1EF, England.

Cover picture by Chris Simpson

Printed in England by The Capernwray Press, Carnforth, Lancashire.

Contents

Foreword 5

Preface 6

The Early Years 7

Learning from War 11

The Rock 15

My Call to Preach 19

"What a God!" 25

Difficult Days 31

Taking up the Challenge 35

Sunbridge Road 43

Experiences in Ministry 51

Testimonies of Grace 63

Mission World! 75

Guerillas, Ants and Royalty 87

Retirement—a New Venture 97

A Well-Earned Rest 109

Postscript 121

Foreword

I count it a great privilege to have been asked to write a foreword for this book, as Pastor Douglas Evans is an old and much respected friend of mine. This is an unusual book as it is written in the form of a personal testimony, showing the remarkable way in which his Lord has directed his life. I have often jibed when the word "I" has been repeated in a book, but Pastor Evans is a truly shy and humble man and he in no way intrudes as he seeks to bring honour and glory to the name of the Lord Jesus.

Pastor Evans has had a remarkable and exciting life: army experience as a gunner during World War II, the loss of his first wife, financial pressures, the running of a large mission, and world-wide travel, often in dangerous circumstances. I am particularly struck by the way in which every experience that he went through prepared the ground for the next one. One of his gifts was in handling many very difficult spiritual counselling problems, including demonology.

He is truly an evangelist and has been used to lead hundreds of people into a personal knowledge of the Lord Jesus Christ. He has a lovely sense of humour, which frequently comes out in this book. Whilst being deeply spiritual, he is very practical and down to earth. When he did have any spare time, and that was very seldom, there was nothing that he enjoyed more than fishing. Although he was very effective at this, I think that this book proves that he was even more effective as a 'fisher of men'!

This is a humbling book. There are perhaps comparatively few people who have dedicated their lives more fully to the Lord Jesus Christ. May many of us determine to follow in the footsteps of Pastor Evans.

Rev. Nick Carr

Preface

I have had a very eventful life and I have travelled to many wonderful places in my ministry, both in this country and overseas. I have made a great many good friends, and it is these friends who have asked me to commit to paper the many wonderful things the Lord has done for me and through me during that ministry.

W Douglas Evans

1
The Early Years

I was born February 10, 1919, in a room over the Moss Shop in Gwersylt, North Wales. The Moss Shop was a grocer's and village store and belonged to my maternal Grandfather Thomas. My parents were George Evans and Jemima (formerly Thomas). My father had come from a farming family in Mold and as they started out on their married life they were reasonably well off. I was the third of ten children of whom five are still living, two boys and three girls. Three of my siblings died in infancy.

The early memories I have of my life in Wales make me think that I cannot have been an easy child to care for. Even in my very early years I managed to get into more than my fair share of trouble, usually with the aid of my sisters and brothers. My father's hobby was breeding rabbits for their fur and I remember being told on one occasion, that my sister May and I, then aged two and one respectively, were lost for some time. We were finally found in the rabbit hutch eating Virol flavoured with rabbit droppings. And still we survived!

I used to love being taken to the blacksmith's forge to see the horses being shod. On one occasion, Grandfather Thomas had taken me there and I was floating things in the barrel of cold water that was used for dousing hot irons. I fell head first into the barrel. Grandfather pulled me out feet first. My lovely dark curly locks were coated with iron filings from the bottom of the barrel and had to be shaved off.

I was sent, with my brothers and sisters, to the Band of Hope. We really looked forward to the Band of Hope Meetings. We sang choruses and we were told about the evils of drink and how to live a moral life. We signed the pledge at one of those meetings. We also went to Sunday School. I can remember being very impressed when one of the teachers read John Bunyan's "Pilgrim's Progress" to us. We went on Charabanc trips to Rhyl from Sunday School. The boys used to fish for crabs with a piece of meat on a length of string. When we caught one we used it to frighten the girls as we chased them. I joined the cubs later on but was expelled because I broke a window.

At the age of five I was taken, very reluctantly, to infant school at Rhosddu and later Gwersylt. Apart from the usual schoolboy tricks I spent a largely uneventful school career. That is until the age of eleven. In more recent days I visited a Gwersylt Church where two ladies recognised me. One was a schoolfriend who remembered me pulling her plaits in the playground, the other had been a nanny for my family. Our family was quite wealthy and we always had a nanny.

My father was employed by the mines and during the General Strike of 1926 he sank his own mine. I can remember being lowered down the shaft of that mine in a bucket when I was about seven. My father was upset when the strike ended because he had been doing well with his own pit.

When I was around nine or ten I had a teacher who was very strict. I was always eager to please and one day, after we had had a lesson about snails, I collected a large paper bag full of snails to give to her. When I got to the class room she was not there so I lifted the lid of her desk, popped in the bag of snails, and went out to the playground to play. When the teacher opened her desk there was a loud scream of horror. She asked who had brought the snails. I proudly said that I had done so. I was smacked for my pains. But I got my own back. The same teacher decided to put on a play for the school. The play was a very serious drama and my part was that of a doctor. I was to wear a top hat and carry a Gladstone bag. I was to open my bag, produce two tablets and say, "Take these two tablets and you should feel better soon." At the actual performance I opened the bag and produced two tennis balls instead of two tablets. The teacher was less than pleased when the drama disintegrated into a farce but the audience loved it.

Shortly after this incident my family moved to Manchester because there was no more work for my father in the mining industry. We stayed in a small semi-detached house with an aunt until we found our own accommodation. We were very crowded but we managed. Imagine the cultural shock to young children who had been brought up in the relative peace and quiet of the Welsh countryside. Here we were in a very large city where dreadful things could, and probably would, happen. We heard stories of kidnappings and we were very fearful of being abducted, but we made our own preparations to protect ourselves and our sisters. Each morning my brother Herbert and I loaded our pockets with stones to throw at anyone who looked as if they might be going to take us away. We kept the stones in a secret place in the garden each night and loaded up our ammunition each morning before going to school. Even as a child I was always involved in sport. Boxing, cricket, football (I was a goalkeeper), but my favourite pastime was running. I found it very difficult to run very far in Manchester. All I could do was run round and round the block, which annoyed the neighbours. One lady threatened to throw a bucket of water over me if I didn't stop running past her house.

I stayed at school in Crumpsall until I was fourteen and then I was employed by Timothy White's and Taylors as a trainee dispenser. I used to go to night school in the evenings for training in accounting. In those early days of adult education if a student passed the exam at the end of the year's lessons he or she was given free tuition for the following year. I got two free years because I had a natural ability with figures. However, I was unable to pass the necessary Chemistry exam to enable me to qualify as a dispenser and because an unqualified dispenser cannot get very far, Timothy White's and Taylors and I parted company when I was eighteen. During those years my brother Herbert and I, together with sisters May and Phyllis, learnt to dance at the local ballroom. We used to go there as often as possible. The girls always paid for themselves. Of course, we only allowed them to go with us so that we had no need of girlfriends. Girlfriends can be expensive. I once took a girl to the cinema. We sat in the best seats and it cost me a shilling (5p). I still regret spending that shilling. There was so much more that I could have done with it. I could have paid four visits to the cinema on my own, sitting in the cheaper seats of course.

After I left Timothy White's I was offered a trainee position with the Maypole chain. I wasn't there long before the war came. I was called up with the first batch of conscripts. Herbert was already in the Territorial Army and was called up before me.

2
Learning from War

I did my basic training with the Royal Artillery at a barracks in Chester. Now I was Private 1512469 Evans W.D. I was trained on an anti-aircraft gun and with an instrument called a predictor. Information was fed into this predictor about the plane involved, weather and prevailing wind conditions and the gun did the rest. I picked up this skill very quickly because of my ability with figures. At the end of the training period I was sent, with another two gunners, to an Officer Training School in Shotton, Flintshire, having been promoted to Lance-Bombardier. I had no knowledge of, or even interest in, military matters. Like many other young men at that time I didn't even want to be a soldier, but I made the best of it because of the situation with the war. Only one of the three passed the training (and it wasn't me). The other two of us were sent back to our original unit in Chester to find that in our absence the rest of our intake had been posted overseas to Singapore. We felt that we had missed out on what we thought was an easy posting. We found out later that very few of those men survived the Japanese invasion. We were the lucky ones for the moment.

I spent my 21st birthday in February 1940 in a Nissen hut in Wales. The guns had blown out all the windows. It was a terrible winter that year. We had to break the ice so that we could shave. It was very good preparation for what was to come.

I was then given the job of drill instructor under a sergeant, but that didn't last long. I was posted to Deepcot near Aldershot and linked up with a Royal Artillery regiment that was going to Norway. At that point we thought we had the worst possible posting. We were so right.

We set sail from Glasgow in a troopship in the company of

some French alpine skiers and some members of the French Foreign Legion. We sailed round the north of Scotland in order to avoid enemy submarines and very soon we ran into a terrible storm which I thoroughly enjoyed at first. There were only six of us at breakfast each morning. The storm was so ferocious that even the ship's crew were sick. When we came out of the storm we were not far from the fiord that was our destination, which turned out to be Harstad Fiord. I went to the washroom that morning to shave before we disembarked and stepped into a room full of vomit. That morning I was sick for the first time. I was still sick when we landed.

Shortly after we disembarked, but before we had unloaded all our guns and ammunition, an enemy plane bombed our troopship and it was totally destroyed.

There we were in a foreign country, facing an uncertain, possibly nonexistent, future with little or no protection.

Three regiments had disembarked at Harstad from that ill-fated ship – our regiment of Royal Artillery, the French Legion detachment and a regiment of alpine troops. We dispersed into the mountains overlooking Harstad harbour. The designated job for the Royal Artillery was to set up a battery of six guns to protect the harbour from German attacks. We soon discovered that the German attacks came regularly every hour, day and night. This being the 'and of the midnight sun', during the summertime there was plenty of light to aid the attackers. Naturally we now put into practice the gunnery training we had received in North Wales. I can vividly remember feeling very sick when we shot down our first plane, and watched it crash into the fiord. After the first it became easier.

Our battery was machinegunned regularly. One day two men, twenty-one-year-old twins, were killed; handsome young men and friends of us all. Somehow their deaths affected me deeply and still do to this day. I remember that occasion with great sorrow.

Every day on the battery we had to take it in turn, in small groups, to go down to the harbour to get ammunition from a ship. One day when I went down we were wearing full uniform with greatcoats plus arctic overcoats because it was extremely cold, even though it was summer. Whilst carrying the ammunition off the ship to load on to our truck, we became rather warm in our heavy coats. We removed them and piled them on the quayside. On the hour, as the bombing started, all the ammunition party dived for cover except the poor unfortunate soldier who was on duty by the coats. I was on duty that day when the bombing started. I was standing with my back to the ship watching an oil storage tank going up in flames when a terrific bang shook the quayside. I thought a bomb had hit the ammunition ship. I threw myself on the floor and shouted for my mother. I expected to find pieces of ship all over me at any moment, but it never happened. When I collected myself I discovered that the crew on the ammunition ship had decided to have a go at the bombers and were firing their ack-ack guns. I jumped up rather sheepishly and resumed my guard duty.

This stand above Harstad only lasted a few weeks. We were given the order to withdraw. We had to destroy all our guns and throw them into the fiord. We had been sleeping in local farmhouses so we were able to get axes and saws to destroy all the tyres on the vehicles to render them useless to the enemy when they eventually arrived.

We had been on 'iron' rations—a very hard lump of chocolate which was packed full of nourishment. We ate about two blocks a day and nothing else for a week. After the fall of France in 1940 the supply ships still had not arrived, but we managed to get down to Harstad and lie low in the hope of being rescued from the sea. The fighting was quite close, just over the ridge and down to Narvik. We had one rifle to seven men and not many places to go. Eventually a destroyer sailed into the fiord picking up survivors. The vessel came in as close as it could and we were able to climb up ropes on to the ship, all the time under fire from the enemy. I cannot remember to this day what happened to our greatcoats; they just seemed to disappear.

We were suffering from sheer exhaustion through lack of sleep, food and through fear. Time seemed to be telescoped into minutes. We had been in Norway for two months but it seemed like two years. Our journey home seemed short in comparison. We had to transfer from the destroyer to a liner in mid ocean. It was a tricky manoeuvre, involving holding onto a rope while the movement of the sea and the men on the liner hauled us up the side to safety. After all these years it seems a blur. I cannot imagine that I could ever have been that young man who fought, starved, and finally escaped from the horror of that campaign. When I visited Norway in 1982, for the first hour or so, I was conscious of looking for enemy soldiers around every corner. The whole experience left me older, wiser and unloving of man and God.

3
The Rock

I first stood on the Rock in 1940.

I had been brought to Gibraltar in mid 1940 with many other soldiers, almost immediately after being rescued from Norway following a gruelling campaign. We were only allowed four days leave in order to see our families, and then we were to be given new postings. I went home to Manchester, knocked on our front door; my mother opened it and fainted into my arms. Apparently my brother and I had both been posted missing, believed killed, during the same week. The shock of my unexpected return was too much for poor mother. The next day she took me down into Manchester to have my photograph taken with her. She said if I didn't come back next time at least she would have a picture of me. I still have those photographs. What a sight I looked! Skin and bone, and so war-weary. At the age of 21 I was a shattered hulk. Along with many men of my generation I became an old man in one day. To bury friends as young as oneself and then go on with trying to survive attack after attack, bombardment after bombardment, was a very hard lesson to learn. I managed to do it but at great cost to body and soul. After being brought up in a Christian home with good principles I had seen my world shattered before my eyes. I had become not just an agnostic, but an atheist. How could there be a God if He allowed such horror to take place? This horror had a long time to run had I but known it. 1945 was a long way off, but God had work to do in me before peace came again.

On the Rock of Gibraltar we drowned our sorrows and our memories with drink and mindless gambling. We could buy wine very cheaply in the town and we were often the worse for it. Thank goodness my mother could not see me then. My saving grace was sport, boxing and running. It doesn't pay to get drunk too often if you want to win. By 1942, two weary years later, our lives were set in a pattern of duty, occasional days off with nowhere to go, and the constant expectation of invasion of German troops via Spain. We knew that we had only hours to live if that should happen. By 1942 I was a hardened soldier and a very bored young man all at the same time.

One night I went to the cinema in the town. I had not been drinking, so I felt able to tackle the steep walk back up the Rock to my battery after the show.

It is a steep climb, the road rising 1000 feet in a very short distance. Trudging along I was joined by another soldier, an older man who was a cook in another battery. Arthur Perrin was a Baptist lay preacher and secretary of a Baptist church back home in London. This I learned later for we became firm friends, but that night I was horrified when he started to talk about religion!

After a while I began to feel that this man needed guidance. I thought he was some sort of fanatic and I was going to put him straight. Didn't I know that God did not exist? I knew that there was no life after death – 'when you are dead you are done for' was my motto. Wasn't even the Church starting to say that the Bible was not to be trusted? I'd show him that science had more to offer than religion! So we talked: I challenged him, he challenged me, on and on, up and up to the top of the Rock. As we parted company I was sure that I had helped him to see the folly of religion.

A fortnight after that first meeting he appeared suddenly at my side as I was once again walking up the Rock to my billet. I felt that he had been looking out for me. Then of course we had to start another debate about religion. I had lost all interest in the talk we had had two weeks previously and I really did not want to carry on the debate; but he was a very determined man and he did nearly all the talking. I was only half-listening to him but when he had left me I began to ponder on two things that he had said to me. First of all he had said that Jesus was coming back to this world again, and secondly, he said to me that every man and woman born into the world since Adam would have to kneel down before this Lord Jesus and ask for mercy and repent. If we did not do this now we would have to kneel in fear and trembling before the Great White Throne of God and be judged for all the sins we had committed.

Now, I had been brought up in Wales and most of the people in Wales were what you might call Christian and religious. I had been sent to Sunday School but I had never heard these things before. If I had been told these stories then, I had not taken them in, for I knew nothing about the things that Arthur Perrin had told me. I began to think more and more about the things that he had said to me. I resolved to get a Bible and read what it said on the two subjects about which Arthur had spoken.

I was an NCO, and as such I ordered men about. I had also been very successful in the army boxing team and I did not want any of the other men to see me reading a Bible or indeed, even picking up a Bible from the table where books for the men were kept. I managed to find a very small Bible on the table and contrived to hide it from my comrades. I went to a quiet spot on the Rock to read it. I found when I opened it that it was a Church of England Prayer Book.

I began to read. I will always remember thinking that the Bible had got religion in it. I eventually came across Psalm 51: 'Have mercy upon me, O God, according to Thy lovingkindness; according to the multitude of Thy tender mercies blot out my transgressions. Wash me thoroughly from my iniquity, and cleanse me from my sin, for I acknowledge my transgressions: and my sin is ever before me.' At that point I stopped, knelt down and said, "Lord, if there is a God please do this for me." In a way in which I couldn't ever hope to explain I knew at this point that God had answered my prayer, and I sat for quite some time before moving. I found from that moment that I had no desire for drinking alcohol or gambling. I no longer wanted to be involved with the boxing team and I no longer used bad language. The only thing that I did not give up was smoking my pipe, but I would not smoke on Sundays. Eventually, of course, I was advised by my friend Arthur that what you do not do on Sundays you shouldn't do any other day of the week. There was then a complete transformation in my life. I can only say that this was a miracle worked for me by the Lord.

When I got back into the barrack room the men were just about to get into bed. As NCO, I was in charge of the men in that room and I spoke to them about my change of heart. "I want you to know that I have become religious." I turned round and walked out of the room and did not go back until after dark. There then started a great battle. When they realised that it was genuine they started to take advantage, knowing that even though I was an NCO I would not charge them for making fun. I became known as 'Holy Joe'.

One prayer that the Lord did not answer was to my benefit. The NCO's had the privilege of choosing their bunks. Because there were a lot of bugs we usually chose the top bunks so that the bugs would bite the men in the bottom bunks. I wanted the Lord to tell me to give my bunk to the young man underneath. But he did not. The Lord was good to me.

I was to kneel down and pray at the side of that bunk from then on, and the first soul the Lord ever gave me was the man in the bottom bunk. The Lord gave me the grace and the strength to be able to pray by every bunk I ever slept in, right up to the end of my army career. When I was in a very tough training school, as a training sergeant I was still able, by the power and grace of God, to kneel and pray. My army life had now taken on a new direction. I had been asked to work in the battery office as a kind of quartermaster for rations and various other things. I enjoyed this work, typing letters and orders with one finger. I was very sorry when I had orders to go back on the guns again. Those trained on the guns were peacetime soldiers, and had been sent home. We were the next in line to take on these responsibilities. I was sent on a course that was to prove very valuable to me during the rest of my army career. I was to be trained as a gunnery instructor. I was very proud to pass the course on two occasions with 80 points out of 100.

I believed now that everything I did should be to the glory of God.

4
My Call to Preach

I used to go down to the Methodist church in the town at the bottom of the Rock. The Chaplain there, a Major Brown, was a wonderful man of God. He was Chaplain of the nonconformist churches. He took me under his wing and told me of many of his exciting experiences when he had been a Minister in Spain. He taught me a lot, and on Sunday nights gave me the job of leading worship by way of picking the hymns to sing. Major Brown asked me to help him set up a club on the Rock for other soldiers to use in order to be able to witness to them. I was not able to accomplish this because I was returned to the U.K. The club was finally set up and is now in existence in Britain as "The Gibraltar Club." We have regular newsletters and a yearly gathering.

My journey home was quite an experience, an exciting chapter in my life. The "Samaria", one of the great steam liners, had damaged her hull during the landings in North Africa. A gunnery crew was needed to take her home. All men who were eligible for home leave were given the opportunity to volunteer to man the "Samaria" on her home journey. I volunteered and was put in charge of six gunners. It was only when we were well out to sea that we found out what we had let ourselves in for. The ship had a damaged screw so was only able to travel at eight knots. We became part of a slow convoy. She was the biggest in the convoy and as such was an obvious target for enemy aircraft or submarines. However the Lord was with us. Fortunately a great storm blew up in the Bay of Biscay and this protected us from enemy attack. The captain took the ship steadily through the storm and brought us safely home to Liverpool harbour.

I was then faced with another great challenge. I was responsible for seeing that the gunnery crew had transport to London to the Artillery Headquarters. There they could report in and then travel to their homes all over England to see wives and families they had not seen for three years. I had made a promise to God that if I got home safely to Liverpool the first thing I would do would be to go into a church and give thanks. I told my men about my promise and I also told them that I trusted them to be at Lime Street station at a certain time to travel to London. I went to the only church that was open. I saw nuns in the church and realised that it was a Catholic church, but that didn't seem to matter. I sat at the back of the church and gave thanks to the Lord for bringing me home safe. I went back to Lime Street Station at the appointed time and every one of my men were there to meet me. So I saw that the Lord looks after all matters, both great and small.

I finally arrived home on leave. What a wonderful thing it was to see my mother and father. My two brothers were also in the war. Herbert, who was one year younger than me, had been in German hands for some time. Another brother, Haydn, had been wounded and had been in hospital in Italy. This was only the second time I had managed to get home on leave since joining the army in 1939. My parents saw a great change in me, particularly when I would say grace before a meal. I heard my mother saying to my sisters, "Don't worry about him. He's been in Gibraltar a long time and it was hot out there. He will be alright when he gets accustomed to things." Poor Mother. Bless her.

My leave was soon over and I was given a posting to the gun batteries on the East coast. The Home Guard made up the gunnery team of these batteries and regular soldiers attached to each battery were to guide, advise and train. We would travel from one battery to another right up the coast from Grimsby to Hornsea, Scarborough and Redcar. The first thing I always did when I reached a new town was to look for the church that had the best notice board; by that, I mean the church that had the Bible study and prayer time. Thereafter I would worship in that church while I was in that town.

My base was at Hornsea. The Primitive Methodist Church there was a wonderful place. There were some godly old gentlemen there who used to pray down in the basement of the church, and I used to pray with them. Actually, I mostly listened to their prayers. How close they were to the Lord and how good it was to be in their company, to receive so much knowledge of the Lord and of the Word of God.

It was in Hornsea that I met Olga Turner, who was later to become my wife.

Olga was a beautiful young lady. She had been converted at the age of sixteen and had great faith in the Lord. She was a gifted pianist and organist and had a wonderful singing voice. She lived at home caring for her elderly parents. I met them after my first Sunday evening service when they invited me for supper. I readily accepted, only to find that Olga had gone out somewhere else. I drank tea with Mum and Dad and tried not to show my disappointment that Olga was not at home.

Gradually we got to know one another. Her parents even gave her permission to come to the camp open day on condition that I escorted her home. Our friendship developed slowly into love. We both felt that the Lord was blessing us and that a marriage would eventually take place. Actually our courtship was carried on by post as so many relationships were in those sad times. To receive regular letters from Olga was exciting in itself as I had never had a girlfriend, or even a pen friend, before. We really saw very little of one another, both before and after our marriage, until the war ended.

We were married on March 8, 1944 at Hornsea Methodist Chapel. I can only remember two things about our wedding. Olga looked as beautiful as ever and I had a cut lip. The day before I had been carrying the wedding cake to the reception hall when I saw some children playing with a rope round a lamp-post. I put down the washing basket containing the wedding cake and joined in the game, getting my just reward by bumping into the lamp-post and cutting my lip. Looking at our wedding photo brings all this back to me very clearly. After the reception we went to Scarborough for a week's honeymoon.

As D-Day approached all leave was cancelled and we did not see each other again for six months. Here prayer and the presence of the Lord kept us close and very much in love.

I also remember Hornsea in another way. I was able to help with the Sunday School—not just to teach but in helping to keep the children quiet. One night each week I would take the children to the park. I would bring some equipment from the battery and we would have a tug-of-war and play other games. I can remember getting into trouble with the secretary of the Temperance work in the church. We were walking down to the park and I had the children singing "Roll out the Barrel". She didn't appreciate that at all. Neither did I when I realised what the song was about!

I was asked to help to train these children for the Sunday School Anniversary. I was so thrilled. This was my first job, my first opportunity to do something in a church and I was very excited about it; so you can imagine my feelings when I read on the battery notice board that some people were to be sent to the Lake District on the very day of the Sunday School Anniversary, and saw my name at the top of the list. I was to go to a Gas School because I was a gas instructor and we had to be kept up to date with what was happening in the war.

I was so disappointed. I decided to pray to the Lord and ask him to take my name off the list and put it on again a fortnight later so that I would be able to take the Anniversary service. I prayed in earnest but all to no avail. My name was still on the list. I was quite taken aback because the Lord had done so many wonderful things for me prior to this date. However I kept on praying.

When it got to the Friday before the Anniversary I was quite desperate because my name was still there on the notice board. I went and knelt in the special place that I had for praying, and as I knelt there I felt the Lord say, "Let me talk, please." I realised then that I had been crying out for the Lord to help me but I had never listened to Him. He made it clear to me that it wasn't the army that was sending me away. It was the Lord himself who was sending me to preach in Glenridding. I was quite worried by this. I had only once given a testimony in public before and I didn't remember much about it because I had been so nervous. Here the Lord was saying I was going to "preach"! But when the Lord tells you to do something you must do as He says.

As we arrived at Glenridding I noticed the Methodist Church at the side of the road. It is still there today. I assumed that that was where I was being sent to preach. I thought that there would be ladies serving tea at some weeknight meeting and if I went there and got to know them they would invite me to go along on the Sunday to preach or to give a testimony of some sort. I discovered that there were no ladies giving tea to soldiers. We were in a secret establishment and we were not even allowed out without permission. Nevertheless in the quiet periods between lectures I prepared a message from John chapter 10. "I am the door by which if any man enter he shall be saved and go in and out and find pasture." On the Sunday morning I got permission to go to Church. I arrived at the Methodist Church and as I turned to go up the steps a gentleman standing in the doorway said, "Ah, soldier, do you preach?" What a wonderful experience it was. I still feel it every time I think about it. I knew that the Lord had put me in that place at that time. I was so stunned by this knowledge that all I could do was stutter, "Well I believe the Lord wants me to take a meeting here today."

"Right," he said. "I know a place seven miles away where they haven't a preacher today. I will get on my bicycle and go there, and you can stay here." I preached the gospel in that church both morning and evening.

On my way home the following Sunday I saw a man standing in a queue. He had a Bible under his arm.

I said to him, "Are you a preacher, sir?" and he answered "Yes, are you?" I said, "Yes I have preached."

He said "Good, come with me. I am going to a church and you can give the message." Without telling him that I had preached only once before, I went and gave the same message at a church somewhere between Hull and Hornsea. I still can't remember where that church was.

So God revealed to me His plan: this was my call to preach. I thank the Lord even to this day that I was so honoured.

5
"What a God!"

Now came a change. The second front had established itself and British Forces had landed successfully in Europe.

During this period I went up to Scotland to help with mountain gunnery training. We were hoping to train some mules to carry guns up Ben Nevis in preparation for going to work in Norway where mules might be used to carry guns up to the high points above the fiords. I was on duty one night, in charge of the guard, and on the list they gave me was the name of a man who had gone absent without leave. That was a very serious offence; it still is, especially from a secret training establishment. Wartime security was very strict. Over the years we tend to forget that fact. I was really surprised when the missing man walked into the guard room in the middle of the night. He had just come back from his home in London. It was my duty to read out to him the charge that would be made against him and then put him under arrest. The following morning he would be brought before the commanding officer of the battery after which he would probably be sent to London to appear before a court-martial; and from there to prison.

The commanding officer of this camp was a very tough man, one of the toughest I have ever met. He had a terrible job to do with great responsibility and there was no way that he would ever listen to this young man's excuse for what he had done. He would just have the man marched in before him, read him the riot act as it were, and then have him marched out on his way to London and punishment. This is what everybody, including myself, expected to see happen the following day. You can imagine my surprise and my feelings when this young man said to me, "You are a Christian, aren't you?" "Yes I am," I replied. "You believe in prayer?"

he asked. "I replied, "Yes I do." His next words made me want to run away from him. "Will you pray for me tomorrow so that I get off this charge?" He was challenging the Lord, whom I love. I will always remember that thought going through my mind. I just looked at him and said, "Lie down, get some sleep. I will pray for you." I walked round all night praying in desperation.

The following morning everything happened as we expected. He was marched into the officer's tent. The charge was read out and the sergeant-major was about to give the order to have him marched out again, when the major spoke. To the amazement of us all he said, "Now then, tell me why you did it? Have you spoken to anyone about what you did?" I felt a thrill run through my heart. Yes, God was going to do something after all. The young man told his story. He had received a letter from a neighbour telling him that his wife had run away with another man and had left the children alone in the house. The neighbour had taken the children in and was looking after them but she wanted him to come home straight away to see what was to be done. He had panicked, and without thinking had gone straight home. The major looked at him and said, "I don't know why, but I'm going to let you have another chance. I want you to get yourself off this morning to London to sort out your problems. Do not tell anyone. When you have sorted things out come straight back here. The sergeant-major, who was supposed to give the order to march out, failed to do so; he was so stunned at the verdict that I had to take the man out without orders. We stood quietly outside for a moment until the sergeant-major dismissed us. The young man came up to me and said, "What a God! What a God!"

We all went our various ways. I went walking right out into the lake, praising God as I walked, staggered by what he had done. It was only when I got rather wet that I realised I wasn't a Peter and I had to turn round and go back. I really was so surprised that I had not walked on the water, I felt so close to the Lord. How the Lord God Almighty can do things that seem impossible.

Later I was posted to an NCO School to be trained for special duties. I worked hard and at the end of the course, instead of being sent out on some kind of commando work I was offered a job on the staff. Apparently it was the tradition that the man who passed out with the highest mark on the course was privileged to be given the chance to become an instructor. It was optional but naturally I said "Yes please", and so I became a member of the School staff.

I was sent first of all to a place called Sedgefield, near Durham. The Pastor of the local Methodist church, a man called Charlie Welch, took me under his wing. He had been trained at Cliff College during the 1920's and was very keen on mission work. He told me he was going to show me how to mission. There was a village seven miles from Sedgefield and we were to go there for a week to preach the Word in the Methodist Chapel. He told me that very few people, if any, would come. He didn't tell me how we were going to get there but I knew he would work it out. It was by one bicycle! He pedalled off down the lane for a while and then left the bicycle in a hedge while I walked as quickly as I could. When I came to the hidden bicycle I rode the next leg of the journey and hid it in the hedge for him to pick up and again set off to walk. We covered the seven miles very quickly.

We visited the people in the village and then went round to the chapel. Nobody came, so we had a prayer time together, and cycled home, together. That went on right up to Friday night and he assured me someone would come that night. "It will be one of the ladies who does not agree with this sort of thing. She will be delighted that things have gone wrong for us and she will come to tell us about it," he commented. Sure enough he was right. A lady came just as we were about to kneel in prayer. We carried on with our prayers and as we prayed she was making silly remarks. This seemed to me to be a very strange way to learn to mission. I vowed that if ever I took a mission again I will certainly have more people than this, even if it was only three.

The next night, Saturday, three people came in: a man and his wife and another young lady. We preached the Word and prayed together. We later learned that those three people had started a Sunday School which flourished in a very wonderful way. Praise God!

We then went to Darlington to preach in a big church. We travelled the same way, by bicycle. On the journey poor Charlie had trouble with the brakes and came off the bike. When I got to him he was lying injured at the side of the road but he insisted that I went on to preach. Off I went to Darlington alone. He was to follow when he could. I explained to the stewards at the church what had happened and that I would start the service. I announced the first hymn, then the prayers and lesson, all the time watching the door hoping that Charlie would arrive. We had got to the last verse of the hymn before the message when he came in. I was so delighted to see him.

Then I was moved to Berkhampstead. There was a very large special training school there and I was promoted to Sergeant. The school was made up of people from all different branches of the armed forces. I found that the major in charge of the unit was a Christian. He was a Scottish Highlander and he always wore a kilt. The major asked me which night I would rather have off, Saturday or Sunday. "Sunday please, sir," I replied. "Are you a born-again Christian?" he asked. "Yes, sir," I answered. "Wonderful!" he said, and he shook my hand. I had a lot of difficult experiences at that school because of the types of people who were coming there to be trained. There were army personnel right up to the rank of RSM and Lieutenant, but nevertheless a wonderful thing took place. As usual I went and looked at the notice-board and I was led to go into a Methodist Church in Berkhampstead. The Minister there, a theologian, was a very clever man. He took me home after the first service and we had a little talk by the door. He took me into the attic and opened a box that was there. In the box was a red uniform and he told me that he had been converted while wearing that tunic in the Boer War; so we had a lot in common. He helped me to start studying for the local preachers' exam ready for when the war was over. Later he asked the permission of the major at the camp for me to go and take services in his church every night in the week. The major agreed willingly. That was the beginning of the West Herts Gospel Team. I preached and many responded. By this time we had come to the point where some Americans had joined us. One of them was an opera singer in civilian life. He had been converted before he came into the army. He used to sing and I would preach. We used to have a congregation of between 300 and 400 and what a wonderful time we had. It was very strange to see notices on the lamp-posts, 'Sergeant Evans and the Team. Be here tonight.'

I still have some of those posters. We had the thrill of bringing the Lord into the lives of those people. Through the Word they were saved, not by us, but by the grace of God. Many of those people still keep in touch with us regularly.

6
Difficult Days

When I became a civilian again in 1946 I decided that I would take a course in shop management. This would surely enable me to get a good job to support my family. We had a baby daughter, Jennifer, born in Manchester in 1945. At the end of my course I was given a position in a factory that made rubber soles in Radcliffe. I qualified as a Local Preacher in 1947 and I preached in what was known then as the Radcliffe Circuit. One evening I was asked to take a youth meeting at an after-church rally, at which twelve young men came to the front of the church in response to my invitation. I grouped them together in a team and we started to work together. We would visit any church that would like to have us to work for a week with them. We went round team-preaching each night and God blessed both the work and the team. It was while we were living in Radcliffe in 1948 that our second daughter, Susan, was born.

Olga and I then bought a house in Bury, about nine miles outside Manchester. Soon after, I started work for a large industrial perfume factory, which was a combination of two factories in other parts of the country; but because of transport costs they had decided to bring the two together midway between their old sites. I was to be manager of the factory.

We were now living in the Bury Circuit and I helped to start what became known as the Bury Gospel Team. There were about 150 people in the team and we set about doing team-preaching. This circuit was a large one and therefore it gave us a large area in which to work. Around that time a doctor came home from China. He was one of the last missionaries to be turned out of China when the communists occupied the country! Then there were two other young men, one an accountant and the other a lecturer at the local technical college. We met together to discuss how we could develop this team. We decided that we would finance the work ourselves and that we would have no treasurer. We would invite the local churches to let us use their premises for a week's campaign. We would provide all the literature free of charge and arrange our own publicity. We simply went around the district spreading information about the meetings and we would go on from there. We had a Bible School at one of the churches to enable people to come in and be taught about the scriptures and to understand the Bible.

1954 brought a great tragedy into my life. Olga, my wife, who, as I have already said, was a gifted musician, would help me with the services. I would preach and Olga would sing. One Sunday evening we went to a church in a place called Heywood to a special meeting. Olga was to sing a solo. While we were sitting in the vestry waiting to commence the service she came to us and said she had decided to change her solo for that night. She wanted to sing a hymn from one of the Redemption Books. The hymn she chose was "One day the silver cord will break and I no more as now shall be." She sang it after the message. The wonderful thing about that meeting was that between 12 and 14 of the people who responded to the invitation went into full time ministry, both as missionaries and at home.

The following day we went away on holiday. While we were away Olga felt ill and I tried to persuade her to see a local doctor; but she wanted to come home to see her own doctor, Kenneth Lees. He was a man who was in our team, and a very good friend. I rang him as soon as we got home and he came straight away and diagnosed pneumonia. It seemed that with modern medicine it could be brought under control and there seemed no need for anxiety. I stayed with her, running the factory from home for a week, just popping in for an hour or so during the day. The second week she seemed to be a lot better and could sit up. We arranged for someone to come in to help with the housework for a week. One morning she asked me for her breakfast. I gave her a bowl to wash while I went to get it. I went and prepared egg, bacon, fried bread and coffee. When I took the meal up to her I found her dead on the floor. She had had a thrombosis. I rang Kenneth Lees. He was as distressed as I was. Together we knelt down to pray and our prayers were the same. "Lord, keep our faith. Lord, we don't know why, but in the midst of all that is happening, keep our faith." The Lord strengthened us.

Life then became very difficult. Not only had I a very responsible job in the perfume factory, but I was left with two small girls to care for. Jennifer and Susan were aged nine and six. Olga's sister offered to take the girls to live with them in Hull. I went over there to discuss the possibility of them staying there until they were of an age when I could cope.

On the Sunday morning I went to the Methodist Church in Hull. There was a christening after the service. Both our daughters had been christened in the Methodist church. I heard the minister ask the parents of the baby about to be baptised to promise to bring the child up in a Christian home and give them access to the church. I had made that promise with Olga and here I was about to give them away, as it were, to a home which, although it was wealthy, was not a Christian home in the way that the children would have access to church services. I resolved that morning that whatever happened I would keep that vow. I decided to take them home with me, whatever problems that might cause.

I had a lot of help. Quite a number of the team people from the local church stepped in to help me. One couple, Mr and Mrs Scheldt, were very good friends, and had been from the day that we went to live in that part of the world. They regularly came across the fields to that little house we had just outside Bury. He was the local preacher's secretary and so we had quite a lot of fellowship together. They had a daughter called Marie. She had just finished training to become a teacher and was working in a school nearby. She came along with many others to help with the children. She was very good and did a lot for them. She often came with a friend to baby-sit for me so that I could go to meetings.

This situation went on for quite some time and Marie and I got to know one another better.

Marie has told me that one morning as she was going to work on the bus she heard a definite voice telling her that she would marry Douglas Evans. Her answer, to the surprise of the other passengers, was a loud "Oh, no I won't!"

Nevertheless this seemed to be the way the Lord was going to resolve my situation. Marie and I were married on June 4, 1955 at the Heap Bridge Methodist Church. We then set about building a new life for ourselves with Jennifer and Susan.

All this time the Lord's work was going on. Many, many more people were linked with us. We took campaigns to Heywood and even into Manchester, seeing many people converted.

Then came 1956, the year of Dr Sangster's Presidency of the Methodist Church. He called on the church to use the year as a time of evangelism, himself travelling up and down the country with Tom Butler of Cliff College and many others. They preached the Word and took campaigns; and if you look at the record of the Methodist Church that was the only time its membership went up rather than down. The tragedy is that the figures did not carry on going up. Sadly since then figures have been going down. Nevertheless it was a time of great opportunity. We got together and had a 'Tell Bury' campaign; God blessed us in our work. The first week each church took the opportunity to preach the Word and called the people to do God's work. The second week we had Tom Butler and we had great responses from his ministry. On the final Saturday night we had Dr Sangster himself. We had taken a large army drill hall, and we filled it. The Doctor spoke to the people. Then we took him to a big church near the hall that was capable of holding more than 400 people. What a marvellous occasion that was: there were many wonderful conversions and the whole area was ringing with the glory of God.

Dr Sangster asked me to go into full-time ministry. Marie was prepared for me to do this whatever it cost or however difficult it might be. We now had a son, David, born in 1956, but still she said that we must answer the call. That was the wonderful thing about Marie. She perhaps has not been much in the limelight although she is a dedicated worker and a wonderful speaker.

This then was to be our great challenge.

We had a lovely house, I had a great job. I enjoyed my work at the perfume factory. Another drawback was that there was no way I could be trained. I am a fundamentalist and believe the Bible from Genesis to Revelation. I had read it and studied it for all those years. I couldn't possibly change now. Or could I?

7
Taking up the Challenge

Now a time of change had come. I had never even thought about, much less expected, going into full-time ministry. If I had thought about it I am sure there were many good reasons I could put forward against it. But Dr Sangster wanted me to take up a vacant place at Cliff College to go and preach evangelism up and down the country, but unfortunately, for various reasons, that became impossible. That door had closed, but immediately the town of Bury knew that I had turned down that invitation they took it for granted that I would be available for ministry in their churches. I was honoured, and greatly embarrassed, to have three of the biggest churches in the town approach me to become their pastor. Having worked in all the churches and having had many of the people in those churches come to the Lord under my ministry, I did not think it appropriate for me to take a church in Bury. I believed that all the people who had come to Christ through me would flock to any church that I accepted and that all the work that had been done by the Holy Spirit through me in that town would be undone. I turned down all those invitations.

Marie and I talked at some length about these things and together came to the decision that if the Lord really wanted us He would open another door. We were prepared to wait for His call. We would just carry on with our lives, as it were, and if there was a definite call then we would pray together and respond accordingly. As it happened it was two years before the call came, but come it did.

In the meantime, many, many people were converted. We had great rallies and meetings up and down the whole of the Rossendale Valley. (It was a great experience in recent days to accept an invitation to preach in a Baptist Church in the Rossendale Valley.

All the deacons who were converted in those early days of mission stood up to testify how they came to know the Lord under our ministry. It was thrilling after all those years.)

Then, finally, the Lord opened the door for us. Harry Lister, a Methodist minister and a very good friend of mine, asked me if I would take him to Manchester on my motorbike. He wanted to go to the Evangelical Library which I discovered was in the offices of the Manchester City Mission. I did not know then that Harry had already discussed me with Derek Thompson, the President of the Manchester City Mission, during his visits to the Mission. When we reached the Evangelical Library he knocked on a door and Derek opened the door and invited us in. Together we three talked about the possibility of my entering into the work of the Manchester City Mission.

There were lots of problems. First of all they had no property. We had our own house in Bury but I knew that the price gap between the two areas was a large one. Houses in Bury were cheap compared with Manchester. I discussed it with Marie. I told her that I felt the door had opened at last and she immediately said that we should go. I pointed out to her all the difficulties. We would not have much to live on and how impossible it would be to uproot the family, the two girls and baby David; but she still felt that we should go. I then went to telephone someone who was on the staff of the Mission. I knew he was unhappy about the Mission and I thought he would add his support that it was not the right thing for me. To my amazement he said that I was just what the Mission wanted. We knew it would be very, very difficult, but we accepted the invitation. The Lord had opened the door and off we went through it on our motorbike round the area where we would work, looking for a house. It was not easy to find a house we could afford that would be large enough for the work for which it was to be used. We sang as we travelled, "The Lord knows the way through the wilderness" and He must have heard us: for we found a house on the main road not far from the mission hall where I would work. It was a veritable wilderness. We could not see much of the house because of the overgrown garden; it had been empty for some time because of some difficulty regarding ownership. The Lord certainly does know the way through the wilderness, because eventually the problems were sorted out and this was the house that we bought.

We had been used to quite a good standard of living and we had to learn to live on very little. It was very hard to adjust, but the Lord knew what we needed in every way. The Lord had given us a wonderful opportunity to gain experience that would help us in a Ministry that, unknown to us, was still ahead of us. Looking back we know that we could never have carried out the work ahead if we had not had the experience of the Manchester City Mission.

We found that the little Mission that was given to us was in a very poor, rundown area. We never had more than ten people at fellowship meetings. We used to go out on to the bombed areas and work amongst the children who seemed to congregate there. There were several groups all headed by a 'leader'. I asked these leaders if they could do the impossible. They informed me that they "could do anything". I then asked them if they could get all these young people into my mission because I wanted to talk to them. I could see that they were not very keen on the idea, but they had accepted the challenge. In that way I filled the Mission with young people, hooligans really. They were terrible. But I talked to them, and I marched them like soldiers 'in the Lord's army'. I don't think the people in the church liked that very much, but the Lord had a hand in it. I soon had a group of around ten or so young men who were 'interested', but they were not converted yet.

I arranged special Thursday meetings for them in one of the vestries at the church. At first all we did was talk about all manner of things, but eventually I was able to teach them how to pray. I had to start right from scratch with them. I used to give them slips of paper on which were written things that they could pray about, people or things that I felt needed prayer. At one meeting I came in and found a young boy who was quite upset about something. He finally told me that the gate to the alleyway had been stolen. It had been put there to stop people congregating in the alley and creating a disturbance. The young lad thought he knew where the gate had been taken so we went out to look for it, but without success. By the time we arrived back at the church some of the other boys had arrived, so we told them what had happened. I started to get out my slips of paper with subjects for prayer when one of the boys asked why we shouldn't pray for the gate. The gate belonged to God and they assumed that if we prayed for its return it would be brought back. Such simple faith! We all bowed our heads in prayer. I will never forget that experience. They prayed, "Lord please bring us back the gate." Those words were repeated all round the group. Suddenly the door opened and in came a very tough-looking young man with red hair asking who had accused him of stealing the gate. I told him that no one had accused him but if he had taken it he had done a very serious thing because the gate belonged to God.

I noticed that he had a cross round his neck which suggested that he was a Catholic. I challenged him, "What are you going to say to God when you stand in front of him after you have stolen His gate?" At this he turned and walked away.

I turned back to my little group and asked if we should pray for God to forgive the thief. "No! We still want our gate back," was the reply. Again we bowed our heads and started from where we had left off. Very soon the door opened again. In came a group of youngsters each carrying a bit of the gate. It had been broken up, presumably for scrap. I don't think it ever got put back on its hinges, but it was returned. The youngsters then began to pray again, thanking the Lord Jesus for the return of the gate.

I don't know what happened to a lot of those boys but I am convinced that somewhere in this world they will be working for the Lord. That experience made our move from Bury all worthwhile, as did the work we did among those deprived people in that area of Manchester.

At Christmas time we opened up a small gallery in the Mission and collected all the toys we could, so that we would be able to distribute them around the district to all the people who were too poor to buy their children toys. Most came to the Mission to collect their gifts. Some were too sensitive to come, so after all the visitors had gone, we put what was left of the toys in David's pram, which Marie and I pushed around until we had distributed all the toys.

Marie worked at this time among the women in the community. She helped to clean the houses and was a marvellous minister in this way.

In the fullness of time we were thrilled to discover that we were to have another child. We were delighted when a little daughter was born in January 1962. We named her Cerydwen. At the time our 'salary' from the Mission was paid in a small brown envelope each month and by some miracle the envelope, like the widow's cruse of oil, never seemed to be empty. We received so many acts of kindness from the people in the community.

I had a telephone call from a man who had worked for me in the perfume factory in Bury. He was a distiller, and a very good one too. He used to travel to work every day from Manchester to Bury, a distance of some nine miles. Apparently he had had an operation and the doctor had told him that when he had recovered he must try to get a job locally because the travelling would be too much for him. Somehow he had managed to get hold of my telephone number in Manchester and he wanted to know if I could help him in any way. One of the men who used to be a manager in the perfume factory now held a managing position with a soft drinks manufacturer. I went to see him to find out if he knew of any work that my friend might be able to do. I asked for the manager by name and when they realised I didn't have an appointment they told me that he would not be able to see me either today or any other day that week because he was so very busy. I was about to turn and walk out when one of the chemists came into the office. By good fortune, he also had worked in the perfume factory and was delighted to see me. He also was a Christian and we had worked together in the past on the production of an ointment that we called "Mary's Ointment", named after the perfume that Mary put on the head and feet of Jesus.

When the chemist saw me he wanted to know what I was doing there. He didn't know that I had left the perfume factory and was now in the ministry. He invited me into the laboratory to tell me about the things he was doing now. In the meantime they put a call out for the manager. When he turned up I told him why I had come. He said, "Right, I'll strike a bargain with you. I ought to be out this afternoon but I can't leave the factory with no-one in charge. There is nothing in this factory that you don't know about. You take over for me this afternoon and I will give your friend a job."

So for one afternoon I was taken back two years, back to the time when I was working in the perfume factory. I enjoyed myself very much and when the manager came back he begged me to go and work alongside him. That was a very hard decision to make. Here I was, hardly knowing where the next meal was coming from, and I had to turn down a very well paid job. As I walked home I remembered that we had asked the Lord to open a door for us and we would go through it. No, we could not go back on our decision now.

When I reached home I had a visitor. A minister from the Mission had come to tell me he was leaving. His wife had never settled in the North and they were going home to London. He had come to ask me to take over his hall, which was the largest in the area. That was a very interesting proposition, but about six months earlier he had told me about a visit he had paid to Bradford. He had preached at Sunbridge Road Mission and had been invited to go there as their pastor. His wife refused to go there because she didn't like the North. He had told me about the Mission, of how it was Methodist-based and to me it sounded like a place in which I could feel at home. When he asked me to take over his Mission Hall in Manchester I told him that I felt that the Lord did not really want me in the Manchester City Mission. I told him also that when I heard that he was not accepting the invitation to go to Bradford I began to feel very warm towards the idea of going there myself. I felt that this was a challenge that I should take up.

My friend thought that they had probably got a new pastor by now but nevertheless he rang Mr Jackman, who was President of the Mission at that time, and told him about me. I was invited to go to Bradford to preach for a weekend (to let them look me over). As soon as I arrived at the Sunbridge Road Mission in Bradford I felt part of the place and knew that the Lord had blessed me yet again.

I remember preaching a very strange message on that Saturday night. There were about twenty-four people in a small room at the back of the Mission.

After the Lord's Day services they put me in a small room and said that Mr Jackman would take me to the station for my train. What I didn't know was that the trustees of the church had met together right away and come to a unanimous decision to invite me to be their pastor.

So we entered into the real ministry that the Lord had had in mind all those years ago in Gibraltar.

8
Sunbridge Road

Sunbridge Road Mission was an offshoot from a very prosperous Methodist Church in Bradford. The founder was a Mr Sleight and though he had died many years before I came to Bradford, I felt that I knew him from the stories I was told about him by the many families he had helped.

The Mission itself was built in the mill area of Bradford. There was a great deal of poverty in the area at that time and Mr Sleight had often been known to go into the homes of mill workers to help them financially and in many other ways. The Mission rose from a small building that had been erected to assist in the work among the poor in the area. Mr. Sleight was very interested in mission work and was a personal friend of Hudson Taylor, who came from Barnsley, not very many miles from Bradford. Mr. Sleight and his fiancée wanted to go together into the mission field in China, but he was not very strong, which prevented him from doing so; but his fiancée was able to go. It was intended that she should remain in China for seven years and then come home when they would marry. However, because of the Boxer risings she had to come home earlier; they both worked together at Sunbridge Road Mission. Both of them were very strong in character and in the knowledge of the Word of God. They did wonderful work there among the poor.

The Methodist Church was not very pleased with the way things were happening at the Mission, and withdrew Mr. Sleight from the work there. At this point he decided that never again did he want to have to rely on a building that belonged to someone else. To ensure the continuity of his mission work he began to buy up all the houses and cottages around the building in Sunbridge Road and rehoused the people. He pulled down all the houses and built a new part to the existing building in Sunbridge Road. Because he felt that the Methodist Church had let him down in the past he did not really trust them. Therefore his new building had doors connecting it to the old one. There was also a separate heating system. This way, if the Methodists displeased him, he could lock them out of his part of the building.

All this had happened many years before I came to the Mission, but the Trust that had been set up by Mr. Sleight was still in operation. There is still a group of men, trustees, who make sure that the pulpit is kept pure and free from the inroads of Modernistic Theology.

It was decided that the Mission should have a pastor, although the Methodist Superintendent came once a month to celebrate the Lord's Supper, and at one time took all the weddings and funerals. Mr. Sleight made arrangements for Harry Kilbride to return from London to become the first pastor. Harry Kilbride had been converted from a Catholic background and had gone to work in the London City Mission. Mr. Sleight financed the pastor in those days, as he financed many other things in connection with the Mission. When he finally departed this life to go home to Glory he endowed the church with enough money to finance the pastor for many years to come. That money was still there when I arrived in Bradford.

The Mission is based on the Methodist teachings both in the doctrines included in John Wesley's sermons and in the system of class meetings; there was strength in both these things. The building itself had rooms upstairs where the people gathered each week round their class leader. Because there were meetings every night of the week there was prayer in the church seven days a week. This system of class meetings was in operation at the time I arrived at Sunbridge Road and it still survives today.

Mr. Fred Mitchell was a chemist in Bradford. He was not only a brilliant Bible teacher but a very godly man, bringing great blessings both to the Mission and to Bradford itself. He had been involved in a big way with the China Inland Mission as it used to be called. He introduced many great preachers to the Mission and a system developed whereby the Pastor would preach two or three Sundays a month and other great preachers, mainly from Fred

Mitchell's home town, Keswick, would occupy the pulpit on the other Sundays. These preachers were men of great renown.

When I arrived at Sunbridge Road I found to my delight that a room had been set aside to be the Pastor's study. There was a long table with chairs and bookshelves. Not long after I arrived a young man came forward and offered to pay for the installation of a gas fire. That was very welcome because we did not have the heating on during the week and the extra comfort of the gas fire was very welcome. I prayed to the Lord and asked Him why he had brought me here to Bradford. What purpose could I serve? My purpose was to build up the class system. Over the years men and women have come forward and become class leaders, people who were not only able to teach the Word but were able to watch over the flock, as it were. When I retired from the Mission there were 270 people at class meetings each week.

It soon became clear to me that my task was not to plough but to weed. As a young man brought up in the farming area of Wales I knew what weeding was. Weeding is a slow, careful job, paying attention to detail and removing the weed obstacles that are preventing the healthy plants from attaining their full potential; whereas ploughing, well—all you had to do was to sit and enjoy the ride. I wasn't here to sit and enjoy the ride, I was here to work. I had realised the value of the class meetings, and I set about my task of nurturing them in their growth. I had a lot of problems because the church had been without a pastor for two years. Pastor Ewing had only stayed three years. Since he left there had been a general falling away in membership, just the same thing as happened in all the denominations in England. When I arrived there was a gathering of between 45 and 50 people in the "Morning Room", so called because it was where the Sleights used to do their teaching on a Sunday morning, mainly to men I was told.

I was directed to use systematic preaching and I began that first Sunday by preaching on "The Sermon on the Mount". It took us nearly three years to accomplish the whole Sermon on the Mount because of the system of other preachers coming in to take services.

Soon after we came to Bradford we were overjoyed at the birth of another baby daughter whom we named Anwen. We were indeed blessed.

At that time the Lord put His hand on the Sunbridge Road Mission in a most remarkable way. The morning service began to grow, and it grew so much that we had to take down the partition in order to get all the people in.

I had come to the Mission on a three-year 'contract' as it were. We agreed at the beginning that we would review the situation after three years and if it was felt that I had not been successful then we would part company in a nice gentlemanly way.

There had developed a division among the trustees about my ministry; they decided that I could not be given a further period of time for ministering. I was given a year's probation to try to get things right and make a better effort to improve where I was very weak. I am afraid this news hit me hard and I sat in my study until the early hours of the morning wondering and praying to the Lord to find out what He wanted me to do. I felt that I was going to have to move again and I didn't want to go. I felt excited and thrilled about what had happened, about what the Lord was doing through me. People were being saved and there were blessings in many parts of the Church. But I now knew what I had to do. I made up my mind that I would say nothing to the trustees until the next meeting and then I would tell them that I wanted three years' guaranteed ministry or I would have to move away to wherever the Lord guided me. This then was the message for the trustees from the Lord. But before the next trustees' meeting thing really began to happen. The Lord once more poured out His blessings and the congregation grew and grew. I couldn't believe what was happening. Where were they all coming from? The congregation grew so fast that we were unable to accommodate everybody. People were sitting in the corridors because they couldn't get into the small hall. One Sunday morning, after our first hymn, I instructed the people to pick up their hymnbooks and follow me into the large hall. It was the only way that everyone could be accommodated.

The time for the trustees' meeting came and they were so high in spirits about what the Lord was doing that I was tempted not to say anything about leaving because I knew that they would want to keep me there now. However, I strongly felt that I should share with them what the Lord had directed, that I was to have three years or I would have to leave as soon as a place was found for me to go. They gave me my three years and I must put on record that no minister in the world could have had a better group of men for whom to work. Throughout the whole of my ministry I found only sympathy and understanding. They allowed me freedom to concentrate on the spiritual work, doing all the other administrative things themselves. God blessed us, and multiplied us.

It was not long before the large hall was full; then we had to get closed-circuit television cameras to relay the services into other rooms. We were the first church in the country to do this.

The Church was always interested in mission work. We decided to put up a tent on one of the estates. Although there did not seem to be much response it did bring some blessings. Then we put up the tent in a park and I would like to share with you one of the many stories about the tent in the park.

Among those who responded to the call of Jesus was a couple, both small in stature. They came forward and were counselled. Some time later their counsellor came to me and told me that a visit had been made to the couple at home. The counsellor was rather worried about their home situation and asked me to call and see them. When I paid them a visit I found that they were living in an area where prostitution was rife. The house in which they lived was a house where prostitutes carried on their trade. This couple had three young girls and I felt that this was not a very good area for them to live. Then they told me their story. The council would not give them a house because they were in debt. Before they were converted they were bingo addicts. They gambled all their money away and failed to pay their rent. This was why they had to live in this particular situation.

About a week later I was asked by a local doctor to visit a man who owned large mills in Bradford. This man also was in a desperate state, though for a different reason. Through Jesus, I was able to bring him comfort and help: so much so that he said that if there was anything he could do to help me, he would. I told him about the couple and he went to a drawer, taking out enough money to pay off the couple's debts. I went straight down to the council offices to pay off the rent arrears. When the people at the council offices heard the name of the people for whom I was paying the debt they told me that there was no way that they could give them a house. Obviously they thought that the couple would get into debt again very quickly. I was shown into another room and there I started to tell the council official that this couple were now different people. They had been converted. Eventually after some talking I paid off the debt, got the rent book signed and took it to the couple. When I presented the book to the lady she sat down and cried. At first I thought it was a cry of delight but I soon realised that it was a cry of anguish. When I finally got the whole story from them it turned out that not a thing in the house was theirs, not even a spoon. They literally had nothing. This might have been a problem, but church people are very generous people. I put the problem to the people at the Mission and when at last the couple were given a house, it was furnished for them, all through the good-hearted people of Sunbridge Road Mission. That couple are still in the Mission today. Great troubles have come and gone but the Lord has upheld them through everything.

That is what it is all about. We went out into the community, and when we went out we were backed up by a fellowship that would pray and help and give.

I was asked to go to the home of a young mother with a sick baby. She told me that the baby was not expected to live because it would not feed. They had tried all kinds of ways to get it to feed. That mother was there walking up and down with the baby in her arms, waiting for it to die. I looked her in the face and asked her if she believed that the Lord Jesus would heal her baby. She believed. I took the baby from her and very soon it went to sleep. Within half an hour it was awake again and taking nourishment. That little baby is quite a big boy now.

As time went by we started to get involved with the people of the town. The Church was very keen to back and support campaigns in the town. I knew that the treasurer would back us all the way and so we found we were contributing the blessings that the Lord had given to us, to the city itself.

We started to hold campaigns in the city and a committee was formed to organise them. The Evangelical committee was made up of a representative, usually a minister or pastor, from each denomination concerned with the campaign. I was chairman of this committee. There was one occasion when a famous speaker had been invited to preach to us at a week-long campaign in the city centre. The representatives of the denominations were all gathered at a meeting to learn how the arrangements were progressing. I had to break the news to them that unfortunately the expected speaker was unable to come. There was a young Baptist minister not very far from me, and as I broke the news I noticed a tear run from his eye. He later explained to me the reason for his distress. He had come from a dying church and had been looking forward so much to having an uplifting experience in the presence of that great speaker. Now the chance was gone.

Back in my study, I prayed about this campaign. I was directed by the Lord to gather the representatives of the churches for another meeting. We met in my study at Sunbridge Road, where I told them that as we had not yet cancelled the hall that had been booked for the visiting speaker, the campaign would go on, but in a different way. We arranged that each denomination would lead the meetings for one night in its turn. We hoped to fill the hall each night; and at every meeting we would invite the people gathered there to come to the front and offer their lives to Christ.

The campaign was a huge success. Very many lives were dedicated to the Lord during that week. Despite the initial disappointment when our planned speaker was unable to come we found that God had once again blessed our work.

9

Experiences in Ministry

At one point in my ministry in Bradford there arrived in the city a group of people who had been trained in America for the purpose of establishing what they called "A Restoration Church". They changed their name so often in the early days that I am not sure what their name is today. This group came in and devastated some of the churches in this city. Fortunately, I had been told about them, and so I was able to warn our people before they got established. I think my people thought I was very severe, but I was able to show them that we now had Satan's Synagogue in our city.

Their main purpose was what we used to call "sheep stealing". People certainly followed them like sheep. I can remember being at a meeting in a Pentecostal church. The Minister there had just received the message that these people now had half his church in their power. He was a broken man and he left the city shortly afterwards. Of course we were very anxious that these people should not progress any further with their work. They indeed were the wolves in sheep's clothing about which we read in the seventh chapter of Matthew.

We survived that crisis. I think that although they have put up rather a large building and are unfortunately still with us, their work in the city is not so strong. I was thankful that I had been forewarned about them and that I was able to deliver my flock from them.

Now I want to look at some of the experiences that I have had during my ministry—experiences that I didn't choose to have but which were all part and parcel of my ministry among the people of the Mission and beyond.

I was invited to the home of one of our West Indian families to try to help them through a domestic problem. As we sat and talked there was a knock at the door and the husband of the lady next door was standing there. He asked me to go to help him. He told me that his wife was somehow going mad. He had already telephoned for an ambulance but he asked me to go to see her. As I sat alone with the woman I was conscious of a great evil. As she started to rant and rave I opened my Bible and began to read Psalm 103. I kept on reading. By the end of the Psalm she was almost herself again. I left her then and I heard that when the ambulance finally did come there was no need for them to take her away. The evil I felt was very powerful; I did not enjoy the experience at all.

We had always trained our children to write down telephone numbers or names and addresses of callers as soon as they were able to answer the telephone. I came home one day and found a note on the telephone pad. I was asked to go to visit a certain house in Bradford. I knew by the address that it was in an area notorious for prostitution. I did not recognise the name of the woman who had requested the visit, but I set off straight away. My knock was answered by an Asian gentleman who partly owned the house. I told him that I was a minister and that I had been requested to call at this address. He didn't seem to understand what I was saying but very soon there was a call from the attic telling me to go up as quickly as I could.

Off I went up the stairs, not knowing what I was going to find. When I got into the attic room there were two girls and a man sitting in a chair, the latter at first glance appearing to be dead. If he wasn't already dead he was in a very bad way. Once again I was conscious of a great evil in the room. I slightly recognised one of the women but I couldn't remember having been in a situation where I could have met her. She told me that I had visited her mother in the hospital. Her mother had been afraid of dying and I had been able to help her. She had remembered the change that had taken place in her mother who had been able to die at peace with the Lord.

Then she began to tell me what had happened in the room. Apparently the Asian people who owned the house wanted to make a takeover bid for the two prostitutes and had tried to evict their minder, the 'dead man', who had become very distressed about it. He had got drunk to prepare himself to go downstairs to attack the Asians with a knife. The girls had stood in his way and they shielded themselves from the knife with a Bible. He had snatched the Bible from them and thrown it into the fire, but it would not burn. They rescued it from the flames. He again tried to go downstairs and once more they stopped him. It was then that he had uttered a great cry and collapsed in the chair, not moving for quite some time. I looked at the man and then questioning the girls further, I found out what had really happened to him. He had drawn a circle on the floor, calling on a demon to come and help him to deal with the 'people downstairs', who wanted to take his girls from him. Unfortunately that demon had come down and possessed him. I looked at him and kindly but boldly commanded the demon to come out of him in the name of Jesus Christ. I said this three times. I was relieved to see that the demon left him; he came round to full consciousness and was normal. The girls were so pleased that peace reigned at last. I went down to my car and collected some things: some small text cards which I pinned up around the room so that the girls could see them and be helped. They were so excited about what had happened in their room that night and they promised that they would come to church. I never saw them again. I tried to contact them but they had left the area.

Looking back, it is remarkable the number of times I have seen Bibles and crosses in the homes of people who live in this way.

I had another experience which brings home the truth concerning the ministry of demons bringing people into the house of God.

I was sitting in my front room counselling a student and helping him to sort out some problems. My wife knocked on the door and told me that there was an urgent message to make a home visit. The lady who had rung said that the road where she lived was in darkness, but she would stand by the gate and wave a teacloth so that I would know who it was that needed help. I took the student back to the University and then set out to make my call, fully expecting that it would again be a case of a fighting husband and wife who needed help. Not thinking it would be anything serious, I felt quite relieved when I drove up and down the road and could see no lady waving a teacloth. I could go straight home to bed. However I drove up the road again and then I saw her. I recognised her as one of the ladies from the Mission. She pleaded with me to go into her house. She appeared to be terrified. I went into the house and there, huddled in a corner, was a group of young ladies, all army wives. One of them in particular was in great distress. I sat down and began to try to piece together what had happened. It was a most uncomfortable experience. Gradually I got the whole story. They had been playing with a Ouija board and in all innocence brought a demon into the house, a very strong one too. Apparently the children had not been able to stay in the house for three weeks and the neighbours were becoming distressed because of the sense of evil in the house. I took the opportunity to talk about Jesus and about hell, for they certainly knew what that was like; also about deliverance and the power of God. I stood up and repeated three times the words "Lord Jesus, cast out this demon". At the third time I had the sensation of being shaken, not a nice experience at all. One of the women who had been playing with the Ouija board screamed out in terror. Then peace once more prevailed.

This exorcism had a tremendous impact on that home and on the homes around where they knew what had happened. At that time we had a bus that went round picking people up for church. On the Sunday following this event it came to the Mission full. We were thrilled to see them. Everyone in the Mission tried to make them feel at home and part of things. We visited them at home but within three months none of them were still in church. Sad isn't it, how soon people forget? The lady who called me to this possessed house had no idea that I had any experience of demons because I have never publicised my work in this connection, not wanting to get too involved with this kind of ministry. She called me as the only person she knew who might be able to help.

I could tell you more stories of this nature but my purpose is to share with you what the Lord enabled me to do during my ministry.

Once we had a group of "Hell's Angels" causing a problem

outside the Mission. They were revving up their motorbikes and generally making a nuisance of themselves. Eventually they went away, but to our surprise and delight they came back. Two of them were converted. They came to the front of the church at my invitation. They were counselled and gave themselves to God. They burned their leather jackets with the slogans. Some time later the leader of the gang came to my study. He told me that I had broken up his gang and that he was going to put a knife in me. Fortunately I was still fit and strong and had some of the skills that I had learned in the army. He was quite amazed when I twisted his arm behind him and took the knife from him. I told him that he had better leave before I got really annoyed and I pushed him through the door. When I came to clear my study upon my retirement I found that knife in the bookcase.

One of these 'Hell's Angels" really gave himself to God. He went to theological college, married one of our girls and is still part of that fellowship today.

Unfortunately the other young man went wrong and has been in and out of prison. We used to look after him, wrote to him and the ladies of our community helped his family all they could while he was in prison.

One of our members, a doctor, sent a businessman to me to see whether I could help him. He was on the point of a nervous breakdown and as I talked to him I discovered the reason for his problem. He had come from London. His employers had promoted him but his promotion meant moving to Bradford. He and his wife were unable to settle in the North and he had let his unhappiness get right on top of him. I talked to him for a long time and finally, after I had pointed out all the advantages of his staying here in the higher-paid job, I told him that I wanted him to come to church for three Sundays, in the evening. I told him that he need not bother to contribute to the collection but that he should come. He promised to think about it and went away.

I don't really know why I asked him to come to church as a means of solving his problems. I can only say that sometimes we who worked in the mission often thought that the work of the church was like that of a hospital: a place where people who are sick in mind and body could come for healing and comfort.

I was very thrilled and surprised when he appeared in church on the next Sunday evening with his wife and two children. He came again the second Sunday, and on the third Sunday was converted. His wife told me afterwards what had happened. He had told her that the doctor had advised him to make an appointment to see me. He said he thought I was a foolish man to suggest that he attend church services as an answer to his problems. His wife had asked him how much I charged for my advice. Upon being told that I refused to take any money, she suggested that they try the 'medicine'; so she offered to come to the services with him. He did not stay very long in Bradford, being promoted again higher still. And where did he go? Why, back to London of course! There he became a member of a Baptist church. Through the grace of God my 'cure' really had worked.

One day I saw a smart-looking gentleman with his wife in our congregation. After I had welcomed them they told me they had just come to live in Bradford where he had taken up a position of lecturer in the local university. The next time he came he asked if he could come and talk to me in my study during break periods he had at the university. I agreed and said I would be delighted to see him. When he came to see me he told me of the wonderful experience he had had while he and his wife, who was also a teacher, were lecturing in the USA. He had been in some of the great Baptist churches there and had been in the company of some of the godly people in those churches, who had led him to the Lord. Now they had felt it necessary to come back home and look after their parents. That was why they had come to Bradford. He told me that while they had enjoyed the service and my preaching it was not really what they were looking for.

Now, I had already been to America and I knew that there was no way that English Churches could compete with the type of churches he had probably attended. I asked him what he wanted me to do. He asked if I could find them a church that would be more like the kind they had been experiencing. As he had mentioned the Baptist church, I recommended him to an evangelical Baptist church in the town and away he went. I rang the minister of that church and told him the man's story.

After about two months he came back to my study and

thanked me for my help. He said the minister at the church I had recommended was wonderful, but he was struggling. He thought they might have been able to help but they hadn't really been able to do anything. He told me he was very disappointed at the state of the Baptist church. We must remember he was comparing it with the Baptist church in America which is the biggest denomination in the whole of America. It is nothing to have six or seven hundred, or even a thousand people, worshipping on a Sunday . So I said I could help him, but he must realise that we do not have churches of that size in this country. I then recommended him to an Open Brethren church and again rang the minister, passing his story on. A few months went by and once again he turned up in the study. I had been thinking that he might come back. This time I recommended that he go to a wonderful and prosperous evangelical Anglican church on the outskirts of Bradford. The vicar at that time later became the Provost of Bradford and now has a high position in another church in the country. I rang the vicar and he was quite delighted about it. There were quite a lot of professional people at that church and I was thinking now that the different type of society might perhaps help him to settle down. He was there for quite a while, longer than any of the other places, but to my dismay once again he appeared in my study. The thing that flashed through my mind when I saw him was that I had run out of churches. My face must have shown my despair! He saw that, and told me not to panic. This time, he said, he wasn't coming to ask me to find him another church. What he said to me was: "This church here is more like the churches in America, not as big of course, but the fellowship and the singing—this is what we are looking for. I'm afraid, therefore, we have decided that we'll have to put up with you." We both laughed at this. He soon got into harness and said he wanted to do some kind of thesis on counselling.

I had had the privilege of being involved in counselling in the early days in Manchester, even before the Billy Graham Crusade came, helping to counsel in the Businessmen's Saturday night meetings. One of the leading counsellors, Ross Wrigley, came up to Bury and helped us to train some counsellors. On one occasion while he was in my congregation 24 people responded to the appeal and I had to deal with every one of them one by one. We really needed a system of training so that new converts could be counselled properly. Later I helped counsel in the Billy Graham meetings and still use their system now. Because of this I knew that I would be able to help the professor. I gave him all the material that I could and sent him on his happy way. I felt that he would make a good counselling teacher. He later had a book published on his findings on counselling.

One night he came to my home for a chat. As we talked I remembered that he was without transport; I offered to take him back to the university. It was while I was driving him home that my heart was moved to make a visit to a hospital quite near the university. Some time before this I had been asked to go to the hospital to help a man who was dying of cancer. His friends were very concerned about him because he wasn't a Christian. I had seen him a couple of times and I remember quite clearly what he said to me: "I know I'm dying but there will be people killed on the roads who will die before me, even if I only live six months. I'm an atheist and I'm one of the members of the Communist group in Bradford; I've lectured to them on Communist ways."

I said, "I was never a Communist, but I was an atheist. Shake hands." That seemed to shake him as well as shaking his hand. I gave him my testimony and prayed with him, promising to visit him again. Over the next three months I saw him regularly, witnessed to him and befriended him. Now, on one dark evening I was truly moved of God to call and see him. I asked the professor if he minded waiting in the car whilst I went into the hospital. As I walked down the small ward I could see the man watching me. I saw a change in his face. I went and sat beside him. He said, "I'm glad you have come, I've prayed for you to come. I'm going to be like you, I'm not an atheist any more. I believe in the Lord."

I felt full of joy and thanksgiving that he was now safe in the arms of Jesus, and not afraid to die when the time came.

What a wonderful thing that was. I eventually took the professor home, after we had had a time of prayer together in the hospital car park.

A day or so later our new Christian brother made the request to be allowed to go home to die and I was able to minister to him.

It was a very hard thing to do because many times he couldn't breathe and I had to hold his oxygen mask to his face to keep him breathing. One day when I went to see him he told me that he thought his life was coming to a close. He asked me if I had a piece of paper and a pencil. He wanted me to write down arrangements for his funeral. I was surprised at what he said. I knew he had been talking to an awful lot of people about his testimony. He felt that a lot of men would come to his funeral because he had been a lecturer for the telephone company for a long time. He wanted them to know what Jesus has done for him. Then he wrote out his testimony which I was to read. Then he said, "Of course, I was one of the leaders in the Communist group and some of them might come too. I want you to do me a favour. I want you to try and get me a Rolls Royce to be carried in." I smiled, "Yes, so they would know you were a capitalist." We had a difficult job getting that Rolls Royce. It had to be brought from 30 miles away over the Pennines, but we obtained it. The day of the funeral came and I took the service in the church. It was packed with men alongside the family. A few months later on another occasion, I met a man who was unknown to me. He came to me and asked me if I remembered the funeral of his ex-lecturer. He told me he had been there with another man and they had both become Christians as a result of what was said at that funeral.

Isn't it wonderful the way the Lord works?

There was a little wooden hut near the Mission and in that hut there was a tall African gentleman, very smartly dressed. He had a leopard skin across his shoulder. He claimed to be the eldest son of the Chief of the Ibo Tribe of Nigeria and also a Doctor of Theology. We rather doubted that fact. His name was David Okapara and I often used to stop and talk to him. I tried to explain the Gospels to him although I didn't seem to get very far. One day I went around to see him; the hut was closed and I was told that he had gone away. Not very long after that one of the ladies from the Mission met up with a lady who was in desperate need of help, a lady with two half-caste children. Eventually this young woman was really helped and was led to the Lord. She started to come to the Mission and became a wonderful Christian. She grew very quickly in the faith. Of course we asked about her husband and she said he was on holiday; so we left it at that. We looked after her, and my wife did quite a lot for her. One day we got news that her husband had come back home; so I went to visit them to have a word with him. When he opened the door, to my amazement I found it was David. We looked at each other and he said, "I thought it might be you. What have you done to my woman?"

I asked him what he meant.

"Well, she won't have anything to do with me until we get married properly in church." So I told him that it was up to them. I offered to help them all I could but this was a personal matter. After this he started to come to the church. He came to see me one night and said he wanted to become a Christian. It was very difficult trying to help him because he was like no one we had ever met before, but we did our best. Soon we began to arrange the wedding. His wife-to-be said that her mother and father would have nothing to do with her after they had learned that she was living with David Okapara. They didn't like him at all.

As we were arranging the wedding I asked if her father would be coming. She said she didn't think so . I offered to go with her to Manchester, 30 miles over the Pennines, to talk to her parents and see if we could get them to see what had happened to their daughter and to David. We went over to Manchester. I talked to the parents, who were very distressed about it all, and they wouldn't commit themselves to coming to the wedding. I pleaded with her father as I felt that he should at least be at the wedding to give his daughter away, but the mother was obviously against the marriage. As we left, she said she wouldn't come at any price.

When we left after all my pleading, with her father especially because I thought that the father should at least give his daughter away, the mother was obviously against the marriage; she said she wouldn't come at any price.

The day of the wedding arrived. We found at the very last moment that a banquet which we thought had been arranged at a local hotel would not take place because David had not even rung up to book the room until the day before the wedding. Two very senior government ministers had been invited; unfortunately they declined. Our ladies got together and provided for the reception at one hour's notice, and my secretary's husband stood by to be the best man. Just as the bride was about to go down the aisle her father appeared. That was a great answer to prayer. We switched the flower from the buttonhole of the volunteer "father" into the real father's buttonhole and down the aisle they went. Everything seemed to be going very well after that. I warned David about some of the things he was doing—things that I didn't think were right. It was a case of culture rather than a case of deliberately doing things that he shouldn't do. Then one day we had a telephone call from his wife saying David had been taken away. We dashed over to help her because she was quite distressed. We did all that we could for her. David had been sent to jail for an offence that I suspected he had been committing, and had warned him about. Now his wife had lost all faith in him. She packed her bags, put her things together and told us that she was going away. Nobody was to know where she was. She would never get in touch with us again because if she did she would embarrass us when David came out of prison. We have never seen her from that day to this.

Some time later I received a call asking me to visit a man in an open prison in the North of England. The man was David Okapara. I saw a great sad change in him. He was hard and very difficult. The wardens told me that they had asked me to visit because he talked a lot about me. They hoped that I could do something to help him. I said I didn't think I could but I would try. I talked to him for some time but I could see he was very, very bitter. A week or so later I got a call from the Home Office. This time they wanted me to visit, and give them a report on, a man in prison in Leeds. Once again I found that the man was David. I went to the prison, sad to see him in the inner prison. I sat down and talked to him at some length. I came to the decision that this man could not believe that what he had done was wrong. It was only when I first received the call from the Home Office that I started to believe that he really was the eldest son of the Chief of the Ibo tribe. To be honest, I hadn't believed him about this until now. When I made out my report to send to London, I stated that if the man was who he claimed to be then the Home Office would be involved with him at government level at some future date. My recommendation was that he be set free immediately, but sent home, because he was becoming very bitter. Two days later David knocked on our door. The authorities had carried out my recommendations.

David Okapara became the Chief of the Ibo tribe after his father's death. I have never seen him since that day although I have been invited to his palace to meet his 37 wives.

I will not be accepting the invitation.

10
Testimonies of Grace

I was awakened one night by the telephone. A young man said that he would like to come and get me on his motorbike and take me to his home, because he and his family were in serious trouble. He arrived before I had started to get dressed, so I decided to put my clothes on over my pyjamas. I put a coat on because it was very cold and away we went on the back of this motorbike. It was quite a hair-raising experience. The young man was so upset that he drove the bike by his feelings rather than by the rule book. As we went into the house I noticed a canary and a cat.

This was at the time when a film about the occult was being shown in the city. The reason I had been called was that a young lady there had been taken to see the film by a young man who had given her a rabbit's paw and told her it was possessed. She believed this and she believed that she also was possessed. She was holding tightly to the rabbit's paw and there was no way that they could get it out of her hands.

Now this of course wasn't a demon possession problem, it was something even worse to deal with. We talked for a while and as we talked I remembered seeing the cat and the canary as I had come in. I knew that there were no demons present in the house because if there had been the cat and the canary would have been cowering in a corner. I turned to this young lady and said, "There is one thing that I have always wanted to see—something that I have often seen on TV, but never in real life." Then I told her that a cat gets very scared if it becomes aware of a demon. I asked the lady of the house to bring the cat into the room. I asked the terrified young lady to give the rabbit's paw to the cat. Far from being scared, the cat began to play with the rabbit's paw, tossing it around as cats are prone to do with small objects. The young lady laughed and then she cried with relief.

That young lady was very fortunate. If those people had not been so concerned for her welfare, if they had not known where to go to get help and if I had not known how to help, then she could very easily have ended up in hospital for a very long time.

My wife was in the staff room at the school where she teaches. One of the teachers came into the room and told her that she had just been told that it was impossible for her to have a child. She had been longing for a child for some time. She was in great despair. Then for some reason she turned to Marie and said, "Do you think that if your husband would pray to God for us that we would be given a baby?" Marie agreed to ask me. I was then put on a spot as I wasn't quite clear on this issue. So as it was my Bible School night, when people hungry for the Word of God came to meet with me, I told them about this problem with which I had been presented. We talked about this and finally decided we would pray. In a few weeks time the lady came into the staff room with wonderful news. "Marie, we have some great news; we're going to have a baby." (What she actually said was, "We're going to have your husband's baby, the baby he prayed for.") Marie then told her what I had done and told her that it was a Bible School baby. There was great rejoicing.

Some months later I was asked to go as quickly as I could to the maternity hospital, where a lady had been taken in as an emergency. As I was driving to the hospital I thought of all the ladies of my acquaintance who might be having a baby, but I could think of no-one. As I made my way into the hospital the Lord spoke to me. He told me that this baby would live. That was thrilling. I didn't even know that there was a baby, although at a maternity hospital I suppose it couldn't really be anything else. The sister, an Irish girl, met me. She was very concerned that the baby should be baptised. When she saw me she was quite irritated, because she thought I had been a long time coming. She told me that she thought I was too late; she was quite terrified that the child had died without being baptised.

I reassured her as we hurried down to the room where the baby was lying. I asked her whose baby it was that I had been called to. To my surprise it turned out to be the teacher's baby. We went down into the ward where I saw the smallest of all little humans that I had ever seen, and I have seen a lot of premature babies. At the side of the incubator was a bowl of water all ready for a christening. The sister looked at the baby and touched her.

"She's alive, you're a very fortunate man, you are in time," she said.

Once more I told the sister not to panic, not to worry. "This baby will live."

She looked at me and told me not to be foolish, because this baby was already written off. If the baby had died without baptism it would have been my fault.

She put the water in my hand and told me to get on with it, quickly.

Of course we don't christen babies; we dedicate them, but to calm the Sister down I took some water. Thinking that if I poured water on the child's head it might drown, so small was the infant, I put the water on her foot. I thanked the Lord for the child. I was quite excited. The sister marched me out of that ward and I then went to see the mother and father in the recovery ward.

They were quite anxious to know whether I had managed to get there in time to christen Elizabeth before she died. I saw their faces when I said to them that God would not let that baby die. She would live. They did not say anything. We prayed together and then I left them. I was told by them the next time I visited them that apparently when the sister came into the ward she had apologised for 'that minister'. She told them that she didn't know who he was but he must have been drinking heavily.

The parents of the baby told her that although they didn't quite know what was happening or what I meant, they did know for sure that I wasn't drunk. That baby survived and is a lovely girl. Three weeks later when I was in Thailand the nurse from the hospital rang for me. When she was told where I was she said that I had no business being in Thailand because there was a baby in the hospital that was my responsibility.

After that experience the nursing staff who worship with us said, "You've been turning the medical staff at the hospital upside-down again, haven't you?"

God is so gracious. The baby was brought to the Mission to

be dedicated and then never came again.

Now I want to look at a young man; he is my son-in-law. I first met him when he was in trouble with the police over a car registration. I went to see if I could help him. It didn't come off because I felt that someone there didn't like me, for he got a heavier fine than the person before him for the same offence. My daughter loved him from the beginning, although he was a Roman Catholic. We were a bit concerned about this, and not quite sure what to do. I don't know how it happened, but he came into my office and told me off. I was amazed and just looked at him. After giving me a good telling-off for the way I was treating my daughter he marched out. But then he started to come to church. What a wonderful thing it was when he was converted under my ministry, and what a wonderful wedding it was because he had come to know the Lord.

He is a very dedicated man, very prosperous in his work. He built up a wonderful business using so much of it for the Lord. But he does more than that. He used to be the leader of part of our youth fellowship group. We had a coffee bar set up and one day I decided to use the coffee bar to give the unemployed somewhere to go. I gathered some of the ladies of the Mission together to run it, and I set off down to the employment exchange. Unfortunately, the coffee bar staff were the ones who were unemployed. A couple of weeks later as I was walking through the town, a young lady stopped me and asked where I had been the previous week. Apparently people had been waiting for me at the employment exchange. I'd had an argument with a group of Communists who were giving out leaflets. I challenged them and they attacked me with words. The Lord gave me the victory and they walked away. Apparently people had been impressed by what I had said to them. But still none of them came for coffee. I found out later that the only reason they stayed away was the fact that they would have had to pay more bus fare to get to the Mission than the coffee was worth.

Jim worked very hard in three areas of coffee bar work. He would go out in the highways and byways of the city and bring in the 'lost sheep'. How many have been saved under his ministry I cannot tell. Eventually he went to America. I introduced him to

Arthur Blessit. They got on very well together. He went to Los Angeles and worked on the streets there, coming back full of great enthusiasm, and wanting a different type of worship in our fellowship. (We know now that it wouldn't have worked). He went off with his little group, forming a fellowship which has been greatly blessed. They have built a new church in an area where there is no real witness of the gospel. Many of the young people who have gone there have been nurtured in the ways of God

I have said that my study was in the church, where I was most mornings studying, preparing the Word of God and praying. One day there was a knock at the door and in came a young man, a European. He had been born in Hungary, coming to England when there had been troubles there. He was a Roman Catholic. He sat down and he said, "Sir, can you help me to know more about Jesus?" What a request! He told me what had happened to him. He had been sitting in the Mass and he had heard the Lord speak to him. He couldn't go to Mass after that although he still went to church for two years. Very unhappy, he was walking through the town one day when he met an old lady. I didn't seem to know the lady he described, but she obviously knew me very well. He had asked this lady if she knew of anyone who could help him to read and understand the Bible. She directed him to me and that was how we met. He was a wonderful man, growing very quickly in our fellowship. Eventually he was called by the Lord to go back to Hungary to spread the Word. That is what he is doing now.

Now we come to another man, who was an alcoholic. There were quite a number of these people in Bradford. I used to try to talk to them and help, but I never had any success. One day I was coming to the Mission to go into my study, when I found a man sitting on the Mission steps. His name was Billy. I asked him why he was sitting on the steps. He told me that if he sat there he got peace to his back. I said, "That's wonderful, come inside and you will get peace to your whole body." He used to come in on a Sunday night and our church secretary used to help him a great deal. We did all we could for him in his trouble and distress, in his sickness and even in his death. We tried to help him all we could, but we never saw any sign of Billy coming to know the Lord.

I remember an occasion when a young lady came to live in

Bradford. She was born again whilst with her family in the army in Singapore. The man she had married, while out there in Singapore was, to put it lightly, not a very nice man. He used to go off with other women, buying things in her name and leaving her in debt. How many times she took him back I've lost count of, but we tried to do what we could to help her. The last straw came when I got an urgent call to go to rescue her from a house where her husband had left her. I had quite a job to get into that house and to get her out, but I managed it. We took her in, took care of her and she became part of the family like many others had done before. Many people had lived with us at various times, students and all kinds of people.

Marie had done tremendous work at the Manse. She had taken in anyone who needed help. All were welcome. Many times I came in after a full day's work and found her sitting on the steps with the telephone in her hand. She would push a piece of paper with an address on it into my hand, and off I would go. She more than likely had been sitting there on the steps for an hour or more, keeping someone talking on the phone to save them from committing suicide until I could get there. We took in waifs and strays, and it is amazing the things that she did that were not seen; but her reward will be in heaven.

One part of the work of a pastor is visiting the sick in their homes and in hospital. Quite often we are asked to help those who are dying.

There is a group of people, mainly from the Anglican church, who gather in homes and pray for people who are seriously ill. This society is called "The World Prayer Fellowship", and the members invited me to go with them on a visit to Iona, an island off the coast of Scotland. We were visiting the Abbey there and studied the Word of God together. It was a wonderful experience sitting there in the Abbey, feeling almost like abbots.

When we returned to Bradford I was often called by this group to go and minister to dying people for whom they had been praying. Obviously some of the people they held in their prayers did not recover and I was asked to visit them on behalf of the group. This work took me into many homes and hospitals and also into the lives of many people.

The secretary of the group rang me one day and asked me to go to visit a young woman of around 40 who was dying of cancer. When I heard the name, I realised that her husband had helped us install the cameras in the Mission. I contacted him and told him how sorry I was to hear of his wife's illness. I explained that I had been asked by the society to visit her. He told me that although many visitors had come at first, for the last two weeks no-one had been to see her, because she was dying. He then asked me to visit her because she was convinced that she was getting better. I went that same day. She lived a good way out of the city. When I arrived at her home I knocked and was invited in. She was lying on the couch, and was obviously in the final stages of the disease; but when she saw me she asked if I had heard what had happened. She told me that she had been healed. How do you face a situation like that?

I knew that this lady would realise eventually that I was visiting her because she was dying. When we finally got to that stage there were many tears of distress. I stayed long enough to calm her and to give her peace. I went to see that dear soul every day, singing to her some of the hymns from the Sankey book (these were hymns she didn't know, being an Anglican). I am not a good singer by a long way, but she appreciated this and came to a remarkable peace. She died saying, "Thank you, pastor."

I was invited by a doctor to visit another young lady who was dying. She was living with a man who was not her husband and we felt that he would not appreciate the doctor bringing a minister into the house to help them. However, the secretary of the prayer fellowship also knew this girl, and so the three of us went together, the doctor, the secretary and myself. She lived in a seventh-floor flat and as we were travelling in the lift, the doctor asked the secretary if she knew what she was going to do or say. Had she been led in any particular way? The secretary replied that she had been led to pray for healing. Then he turned to me and asked the same question. I said that though I had prayed about this I had not been given an answer; I would wait and see what the Lord said when I saw her. As we arrived at the flat the man pushed past us and went out. We found in that room the most lovely young woman, perhaps in her very early twenties. She had such beautiful hair. My friend the secretary, being already prepared for her ministry, spoke to the young woman and began to pray for healing. When it came to my turn I knew what I had to do.

I told the young woman that I knew she was dying and that the doctor had told me that she also knew that she was dying. I asked her if she knew what happens after death. She did not. I told her that our bodies go into the grave to wait for the day of "Resurrection and Judgement". Then we have to stand before God and he will run a tape of our life for us, as if on a tape recorder. That tape will show all the things we have done, good or bad. She had lived a very unhealthy and evil life and when I asked her how she felt about that she said that it would be a terrible thing to see. This I said was the 'bad news' of the Gospel. But there was also 'good news'. Then I told her how Jesus came to this world, how he lived a perfect life, and his life was also taped. God gave us a wonderful gift in Jesus, and he also gave us salvation. I told her that if she accepted the Lord into her life the 'bad tape' would be erased and the perfect tape of the life of Jesus put in its place. She told me that she wanted that tape. We knelt down and she received the Lord into her life.

She lived for quite a few weeks after that and I visited her every day with one of the ladies from the church. We took hair curlers and curled her beautiful hair. As we witnessed the decline of her body going into decay, we witnessed at the same time the growth of her spiritual life. I was able to get there when she was dying. It was very difficult, because it was the time of the power cuts during the Miners' Strike. All the lights were out, but we lit a candle and I sat by her bed. After a while she opened her eyes and saw me. I promised to stay with her until the end; to which she replied, "Oh no, not the end, the beginning. I look forward to seeing you. Goodbye and thank you. God bless." She closed her eyes and very soon went to be with her Lord. It was amazing to see; it had an impact not only on the man of the house, but the whole family. They asked me to take the funeral service and they all came. They worshipped with us for a long time after that, but they too disappeared.

I was visiting a barber's shop when the barber asked me if I knew that Mr Smith was in hospital. This man was a very wealthy man and a very important person in the city. He was a bachelor, not that that is anything to be ashamed of, but he had the reputation of being a very difficult man to get on with. The barber told me that his nickname was 'Grumpy'. He also told me that no one would be going to visit the sick man. He asked me if I would go. As soon as my haircut was finished I set off for the hospital.

The man was in a private ward and I knew I would have to get permission from the nurse to see him. This might prove rather difficult because he didn't really want to see anyone. It so happened that there was no nurse around when I arrived at the private ward; so I just knocked on the door and walked in. I told the man who I was and that his barber had asked me to call and find out how he was. I talked to him about all manner of things and then noticed that he had never even lowered his newspaper. He just sat there reading, and only grunted at me. I knew that there was no way that I would be allowed in that room again, so I began to tell him about the Lord Jesus. When I had finished speaking I asked if I could call to see him again. His reply? He lowered his newspaper and said, "You've not done me any harm lad; you can come again," and up went the newspaper again.

I visited him regularly after that. Eventually the hospital let me know that he was dying, and I went in to see him. He was surrounded by his family, who asked me what I had done to their uncle. He appeared to be a different man. It was wonderful to get their testimony to the work of God in the life of that man. I went to him and took his hand. I repeated Psalm 23 and told him that there was no need to fear, God was with him. He gripped my hand and was gone.

The family got in touch with me through the solicitor and asked if I would take the funeral service. The chapel where he was to be cremated was packed to the door with people; there were more who could not get in. The civic leaders and most of the council were there. I knew that they had known him well and had known what kind of man he was. After the main part of the service I told that congregation what had happened in that hospital room. In other words, I gave them the testimony of one who was saved on his deathbed. I was able to bring that service to a close with rejoicing for the soul that was now with the Lord through the power of God.

The people all shook hands with me as they were going and you could tell by the way they spoke to me that my words had had a great impact on that gathering.

We find that the Lord can use us in many unusual situations. He guides and leads us in all we do. All we have to do is follow.

We had a young man from Oxford. His name was Alan and he is now in an Anglican ministry in America. I visited one of the churches where he ministered. He went to Romania to work among the students there and met and married a young American lady. They are now in the United States. I remember the time when he came to the front of the church after an invitation. He looked at me and said that on one side he saw Jesus, and the other side he saw Satan; they were fighting. I was so thrilled that he managed to come to Jesus. He is a man who will leave his mark in this world.

Then there was a young lady with a beautiful voice. We met her at a time of great problems due to sickness. We took her in and Marie spent hours talking to her and counselling her. Eventually she got over her sickness and decided to go to America, now living in Pennsylvania and singing for the Billy Graham team. She came over recently and I was at a meeting where she was singing. She said I was probably pleased to see her go so that I could get something done. We are thrilled that we were able to help her through this difficult time and enable her to work for the Lord.

Many people think, I suppose, that if you get a good pastor and a good working team in the church, it will blossom. That is so in many ways. But a church that is going to blossom is a church that is a place where people pray. We had some very godly people in our fellowship. If anybody was ill and they or their relatives requested special prayers, we used to gather together a few people. We would go to the house and would pray with them; then one of our eldest members in spiritual life would be the one to anoint them. Then we would all go home, not together, but all go separate ways. These occasions were not many, but the people who invited us to go were helped and healed.

I want us to look at one last wonderful person. She was converted through one of our lady workers at the age of 75. Having worked in the mill all her life, she had the marks of strain in her body from working the long hours. Before I came to the Mission I was told her story. She loved to serve the Lord and one day they needed someone to help to stoke the boiler which we had in those days. They gave her the keys, and she used to march down the road swinging the keys and shouting "I've got the keys of the Mission, I've got the keys of the Mission." She was so thrilled to serve the Lord by doing anything. She came to me and pleaded with me to find something for her to do, wanting something that she could do every day to help the Mission. I told her that she could pray for the pulpit area, three times a day: morning, afternoon and evening. I told her this was needed so that when people came to preach in the pulpit they would know that the pulpit they stood in had been well prayed for.

When people came to preach they said that they could feel that there was power in that pulpit. This dear soul prayed for the pulpit area three times a day. Unfortunately she had to leave Bradford to be cared for by her son in Blackpool. She went to her son's home but very soon had to go into a nursing home. We visited her there, not as much as we would have liked because of the distance. Sometimes some of the ladies from the Mission would visit her as well, and we used to go and spend time with her. On one occasion one of the nurses asked me if I could have a word with the old lady. Apparently she was always late for every meal, breakfast, dinner and evening meal. When they went into her room they always found her on her knees, praying. I told them that they couldn't expect me to stop one of my prayer warriors praying. "But she is always praying for one thing, a pulpit area."

"Hallelujah!" I said. "No wonder we still have such great blessings at the Mission." And that great soul carried out her prayer duty right to the very end. We missed her when the Lord took her home. I asked some of the ladies if they would like to take up her ministry but I am pretty sure that they did not get anywhere near to the faithfulness of that dear soul. Everyone of us has a job in the work of the Ministry.

11
Mission World!

The telephone rang by the side of my bed as it very often did. In those days I was called out in all kinds of situations. This time it was a fireman I knew. He told me that the Mission was on fire. I jumped out of bed and began to get dressed. In those days I always wore a stiff collar, and as I was buttoning it and trying to get my tie straight, my wife awoke and asked me where I was going.

"The Mission is on fire," I told her.

"And you are getting dressed up like that?" she exclaimed.

"I see what you mean," I replied as I hurriedly put on my coat. I hurried to the Mission and when I arrived I could see flames coming out from the centre of the building where the heating system used to be. The situation looked desperate. I flew into the building and up the stairs to my study, realising that if they broke the windows and poured water in indiscriminately I would lose all my books. It was very hot in there. The window was smashed and a fireman pointed his hose through it.

I shouted to him, "Hey don't do that, I'm in here."

"What are you doing in there?" He looked surprised to see me. I told him I was trying to salvage my books.

He still had to spray water into the room, but he avoided my books. After wetting the room he left me in my study trying to save my books.

That fire was a great tragedy for the Mission.

At that time in Bradford there were people who would set fires in large buildings. One week they would set a mill on fire; perhaps the next week they would set a fire in a church. A very large Pentecostal Church in the city had been set on fire only a month before.

Five fires had been set in the Mission that night. The worst damage was caused in what we called the 'old vestry'. This was a room in the old part of the building where they used to hold their meetings in the early days.

This room jutted out into the large hall. After the fire I felt rather embarrassed because I had often hoped that we would be able to take down that part to give us some more room in the hall to cope with the increasing numbers of people who met there on a Sunday night. At that time people were sitting all around me on a large platform with a loose pulpit in the middle which looked as though it would fall down if you thumped it, as I often did.

After the fire the Mission was in a terrible state: even parts of the new hall were burnt. The plaster on the walls had turned to chalk and it was possible to push a pencil through it. Unfortunately we could not carry on with the plans we had already prepared because the insurance would only pay for the replacement of the damage. However, it was a good insurance company and gave us a good price for the restoration of the Mission.

Until our building was habitable again we were invited by one of the Methodist Churches to worship with them. Every Sunday we went off to this church and, of course, they were well outnumbered. We had the privilege of preaching there and on most of the occasions when we were there young people were converted.

At last our Mission was repaired and we could meet there again. We had enlarged the place where we did our youth work, putting up a new building which had a complete new look. We had turned the Mission round and what had been the front of the hall was now the back. We had a smaller platform at the front, and the rear of the hall was terraced so that the congregation at the back was raised up. That meant that we could get 80 more chairs into the church. I was very excited one day when a worker at the Mission came to me and said that he thought we could get 84 in if we tried. Eventually the church was prepared for use. In the afternoons, between the morning and evening services, a group of us used to go and stand in that burnt-out hall. We used to have a time of prayer and sing at the end "This, this is the God we adore." I'll never forget the feeling as we stood in that smelly, dark place, but now it was brighter than ever. The money we needed to supplement the insurance for restoring the building just came in. The treasurer and I sat in what we called the rest room for short periods and the people came with their envelopes; even the children came with their money. People had sent back their televisions to enable them to give more money to the Mission. Others even took paper rounds to help. They all came, from the very rich to the very poor; everybody contributed to the restoration of the church. It now belonged to the generation of that day. Before, we knew it was the Lord's house, and we knew that the Lord had raised the money to build it, but now it seemed that the Lord was saying, "There you are. I've renewed the work for you, blessed you and multiplied you, and now I have given this new hall to you." That was how some people felt. It was remarkable. The times that people were blessed by what God had done after the fire are talked about to this day.

But the wonderful thing about it to me was that no members were lost, as far as I know, because of the upheaval. I kept my eye on most people to make sure that no-one went missing without us knowing. It was difficult for some people to get to that new place, and it obviously was not the same as the old place; but everybody stuck by us in our troubles. I would like to say "Hallelujah" to that.

When we returned to our nice new church again, we anticipated that the Lord would continue blessing us; but not only did He continue: He multiplied his blessing, and it wasn't long before the television cameras came out to us, especially on our anniversary days and special meetings, when we had the young people from the Sunday school and the Girls' Brigade and the Boys' Brigade. There was some great work going on among the young people, led by Mr and Mrs Williams. Perhaps we would have 80 or so youngsters in the back room, as well as the congregation. Those were wonderful days. God was so good to us.

It was after our return to the Mission, following the fire, that I was led to give a series of sermons on the doctrines of the Evangelical church. There was much blessing amongst our people during the doctrinal messages, and it was about that time that we had an influx of enquiries about baptism. Now we were an Evangelical Methodist Church and we dedicated our children. When anyone wished to be baptised by immersion, the pastor would make arrangements with the local Baptist minister, and if he was baptising any of his congregation he would baptise any of our people who so desired. I would go, give the message and watch the baptism. One week I rang to ask him if he could arrange a baptism meeting for us; he agreed and gave me a date. He asked how many there would be. When I told him that up to then there were 24, he went silent. He asked me to repeat the number. He came along to see me in my study and said he thought we ought to look at this business, telling me he had never baptised so many in his ministry. He thought it seemed somehow wrong; he thought that we should share the service. So we arranged that we would do that. We did so right to the end of my ministry. Many people requested baptism during that time and it was arranged that when our people took over the Baptist Church for baptisms, I would take the service, preach the message and our president would do the baptism. Over 200 people were baptised during this period.

I explained earlier how the foundations of the church were laid down by Mr. Sleight and his helpers, and that there was a two-pronged outreach. One was local among the people in Bradford; and they also followed the Lord's direction to go to the uttermost ends of the world. Mr. Sleight did that in a most remarkable way, not only by enabling his fiancee to go out to China, but also by giving financial help for the work. When she came back they worked together at a local level.

Until just before I arrived there hadn't been a missionary sent out from the Mission, except to London City Mission, for some years. A young lady had gone out to the mission field a few months before I arrived. She was the first missionary to go out from the Mission. When she came home I often sat down with her and we had good conversations together.

Before I share those conversations with you I would like to let you know what system we used for collection of money to support the missionaries. The Methodists still use the same method today. The children would go and ask their parents, aunts and uncles and all other relations to give a certain amount of money each week, and the results were remarkable. Then money would come in from other sources. Once a year we would go into a back room, a blackboard would be put up and all who were interested in the missionary work would come to the meeting, (a Special Allocation Meeting as we called it), to ask for a certain missionary society to be supported. We would put the names of the numerous missionary societies on the board (I never realised there were so many different societies) and then we would divide up the money we had collected during the past year among the societies we had chosen. Some would have a little more than the others according to the various degrees of distress of the people we were to help. Sometimes some of them would have so little that I thought it hardly seemed worth sending the money, and that was one of the weeding jobs the Lord laid on my heart to do. They were very sincere, these people. They loved the Lord, they loved the Mission and they loved the particular cause that they supported, often privately as well as through the church; so I didn't want to disturb any of that wonderful work.

Other than the fact that Methodist missionaries were paid the same as if they were ministering at home, I knew nothing of what went on in the world outside of Methodism until I came to Sunbridge Road. When I talked to Barbara, the young missionary I mentioned earlier, I found that she had had a terrible struggle to survive. She only had a small gift from the Mission and nothing more. I also learned that she had lost a lot of weight. When I asked her about this she told me that she had been living on chocolate for a few months. That went right down into my soul and I went and prayed about this. Once again, as He always does, the Lord Jesus came to our rescue in a most remarkable way. He held me back for quite some time, and then suddenly the day came: I was watching for it. There had been an uprising in Africa, a lot of missionaries had been killed and many others had lost all their belongings. On that occasion somebody suggested that we give a little more to the African Society. We talked about it, and at the end of the day they decided that they would divide all the money among three of the African societies that were in a desperate position. There was such joy in my heart that it was quite a long time before I went home that night. That was the foundation of what was to happen.

Very soon after that we heard from one of our members, who had been at a meeting in Harrogate to hear about a missionary couple who had worked in Thailand for some time. They had built, almost with their own hands, a Bible college in the north of that country. They had come home in a desperate situation. The wife belonged to the Methodist Church and did not receive much money from them. I do not think that the husband received much in the way of monetary support from his church either. They were in desperate need and they didn't feel that they would be able to go back to Thailand because of the financial situation in which they had found themselves. Again the Lord stepped in. The people at Sunbridge Road adopted them, and that seemed to put a new emphasis of mission into the church: so much so, that it grew and grew, until we had more missionaries going out from the Mission. I will tell you about one of them in a later chapter. The finance that came in was amazing. Towards the end of my ministry I had the thrill of seeing a missionary just returned from the field, receive £1,000 from the church just to enable him to look after himself and his family while they were at home. They were given cars by people from the church. They were given food and accommodation. We copied an American idea of holding a "Shower". We put up a list, compiled by the missionaries, of all the things that were needed for them to continue their work. The missionaries would stand by the table and people would come and bring their gifts, from the little children, who came bringing small gifts like toothpaste and brushes, to the larger gifts from wealthier people. It was a wonderful experience to see all the people helping in such a practical way. Unfortunately this kind of thing did not last very long, because soon after that the missionaries started to fly to their destination. Of course, that limited the amount of luggage they could carry with them and at that time money became more important than practical gifts. Nevertheless a mission committee was called which dedicated itself to the task of raising money; we looked after the missionaries in a way that had never been done before. We were all so thrilled at what happened during that period. No one person could claim that he was responsible for the work that went on. It was so evident that the Lord did it. We couldn't have engineered or arranged the work we did if the

Lord had not gone before us, opened the door and flooded the Mission with the money that was required. We now had missionaries whom we adopted going out to Japan, one of whom served as a deaconess at Sunbridge Road Mission in her retirement. Then there were the Davises who were missionaries in Thailand; also a young couple who went to Thailand from us. There was a young lady who went out to Kalimantan, Borneo. By now we had a flourishing number of workers in the mission field and they had a wonderful backing from the home church here in England.

I was given an invitation to become the chairman for the North East Region of the Overseas Missionary Fellowship. This was a new move that was taking place, to have different areas, each with its own chairman. Each chairman gathered a number of willing people who would form a committee. They gave me a wonderful secretary, a great man of God, full of energy. We were able to get our committee into working order before any of the other regions in the country. I learned an awful lot about mission work with the OMF. We travelled to various Bible colleges to see the students and we also met the missionaries when they came home. We also had the job of interviewing candidates for missionary work. It was a terrible decision when you felt that a particular person was not suitable, but it was a joyful thing when you felt that you had found someone who was made for the work. I used to go to meetings in London once a year and it was a wonderful experience to meet with so many godly men and women who were so dedicated to the work of mission.

I would like to introduce you to a young lady called Barbara Mapplebeck. That was her maiden name, because at the time I first knew her she was not married.

One day as I was about to go home after the morning service one of the ladies came to me and told me about a lady who was collecting hymn books in the back hall. I went into the hall to see who it was. There she was collecting up the hymn books and bringing them to the back of the hall. I went to her and said how pleased I was that she had joined us. She told me that this was her first visit to the Mission and that her own church had closed. She told me that this was a job she always used to do. I told her to carry on with her task and again said how pleased we were to have her there and that we hoped she would make herself at home. That lady was the mother of Barbara Mapplebeck.

Barbara used to come to our Brigade and was influenced by the Lord Jesus Christ. Her mother also came to know the Lord, both growing in faith. Eventually her brother came to us and that only left Mr. Mapplebeck, her father. He was a very tough gentleman, having been a paratrooper, and he had no time for church. Somehow they managed to persuade him to go down to the Billy Graham relays. At one of these meetings the Lord spoke to him and he became a transformed man.

At that time Barbara and her father and brother were all champion cyclists. Mrs. Mapplebeck did not take part in the sport. Barbara was at that time the British, and I think the European, cycling champion. The previous year she had only just been beaten in the World Championships and was preparing to enter the competition again. Everyone was so excited about the forthcoming competition and they all felt sure that Barbara would win this time.

In the weeks leading up to the championship Barbara often used to come to talk to me in my study. I felt that she was searching for something, but I could only watch and wait until she had discovered what she was looking for. The morning came when she came and sat with me in my study and I could see from her face that she had found what she was looking for. I felt that she was about to say something very special.

"Pastor," she said, "I am going to put my bicycle away in the cellar and I am going to train for the Mission."

I have met many people in my time who have sacrificed much for the Lord but this was something special. Here was this talented young lady, on the threshold of world fame as a sportswoman, with a house full of trophies, who was prepared to give up everything to undergo training to work on the mission field. However, her family were behind her in her decision and away she went to start her new life. I went to visit her at the Mission Centre where she trained. She told me that as well as her parents supporting her, the Mission was providing for her so well that she felt rich.

When she finished her training she went out to Kalimantan,

Borneo. While she was there she met a charming Canadian missionary worker and eventually they married. On coming home on furlough they came to see me and when her husband came into my study we immediately felt at one with each other. I used to love to talk to him, and I admired all the things he did. When they went back to Kalimantan her father went out to visit them. Eventually they went back to her husband's people in Canada, where the missionary society for which they both worked had a centre. I went to visit them there. They are now working among Red Indians and other people way out in the wilds of Canada.

We think of Mary Slessor and Hudson Taylor and many other missionaries, now no longer with us. Their spirit lives on in the representatives of our own generation and those of us who have had a hand in their training and have been able to help and nurture them, to direct and guide them, feel greatly honoured to have been entrusted with such a mission.

Now I want to tell you about a young man whose name is Peter Wong. The Chinese students started to come into the Bradford College to study, and amongst them were some Chinese Christians who were very concerned about the inroads that the Communist party was making amongst the Chinese students. Peter gathered some of them together. They went to see the padre at the college and asked whether they could have a room for prayer and Bible study. He said "No". It was a very sad thing for the padre to do but looking back, we were very thankful that he did so.

God often says "No". He can use the godly and the ungodly to bring about his purpose. Soon after his rejection by the College Padre, Peter met a married couple who were members of Sunbridge Road Mission. He told them his problem; they brought it to me and thankfully I was able to say "yes" to them. They were given space at the Mission. And so we started up our Chinese section of the work at Sunbridge Road. I could immediately see how the Lord had given us a marvellous opportunity to help his servants.

The Chinese students could have gone to any other church. The university could have accommodated them, but they came to us and established themselves with our Mission. The married couple who had introduced them to us hadn't been with us long. They were dedicated people who looked after these students in a very dedicated way for many years until the wife was called to be with her Lord. Even now as I write the husband is working for the Lord in Singapore.

The work among the Chinese students went on. They had their own Bible study group, although they worshipped with us at morning and evening services; some of them even came to my Bible School. Since my retirement we have had the opportunity to share fellowship with them in one of the halls that they are now able to rent at the university. Peter and I became very friendly with many of the other people. They were closely associated with Mary Wong, who carried on her father's work. She was the daughter of Pastor Wong, who founded the English and European Society. Because the Chinese students had established themselves so firmly at the Sunbridge Road Mission, they were perhaps not so closely linked with the English and European Society as they might have been. They are still with us to this day and I will mention later on about the blessing that they brought to us, through God.

I used to enjoy their weddings. Very colourful occasions. The sincerity with which they received us at the receptions afterwards was so evidently in the name of the Lord.

So now we had amongst us a Chinese fellowship; but before the Chinese community arrived, and not long after I came to Sunbridge Road, the West Indian people started to come and live in our country, quite a number of them coming to live in Bradford.

First the men would come. They would get a job, then they would get a flat, and then they would send for their families to come and join them. One problem that they had when they arrived was the question of the validity of their marriages. If they hadn't registered their marriages at home, then they weren't valid in this country. The fact that they were not legally married was a great trouble to them. They used to go straight to the Registry Office when the wife arrived and they would go through the words of the marriage ceremony. They would get their certificate, which should have made things alright for them. However, they thought they were already married and, although they didn't object to having to go through the marriage ceremony again, they thought that if they had to get married again then they ought to be able to be married in a church.

The Registrar asked me to go and see him to see whether I could help him with this problem. He asked me if I could help to do this and so I agreed. The couples had to bring a form for me to sign to say that I would marry them within three months. This, then, was how I was introduced into work among the West Indian people. Lots of them settled with us at the Mission.

There was a church that was going to be closed down. We managed to work out a way for them to buy the building on rental purchase and they established themselves as a West Indian Church.

The reason that they really needed their own church was one which we might find difficult to understand. They found the time element connected with our churches difficult to cope with. They liked to start a service when they were ready, not at 10.30 a.m. or 6.00 p.m. They also liked to go on worshipping until they were tired and not finish after an hour or so as we did. I acted as adviser to them. Their leaders used to come into my study with the elders. We used to talk over their problems and I used to try to sort them out. I did all the administrative work, and all the dedications and of course the funerals. I did this for many years until they were able to cope on their own.

There was a survey of the people in Bradford to find out where they lived, what they were doing, whether they were going to church or not, and so on. When they got the statistics down at the Town Hall, the officials were surprised to find that there was a man called Pastor Evans who had 200 West Indian people in his church. Officials came to see me about this. I told them that although the West Indian community called me their pastor they did not necessarily attend my church. I told the officials from the Town Hall that these people had their own church and were in the process of opening another on the other side of the town.

My visitors told me that there were a lots of problems with the West Indian community. Would I, as someone who knew their ways and their customs, be prepared to help a team of people who had been set up to work among the West Indians? They were a police team consisting of an inspector, a sergeant and a policewoman. I was included in that team and was often called upon to help them with problems. I was often called out at night when someone had had too much to drink. I helped a lot of the West Indians out of serious trouble.

I remember one particular evening. A lady, who was a member of our church, was standing in our doorway crying broken-heartedly. We invited her in and she poured out her trouble to us. Her parents had died back in the West Indies and she wanted to attend the funeral, but there had been arguments in the family about who should go. Apparently her brother wanted to go as well and there was not enough money for two tickets. I went to her home and after a discussion it was decided that the woman should go. If her brother wanted to, he would have to pay for himself; nevertheless he decided he wanted to go, and away they went.

When they were coming home, their plane was diverted, and they managed to get themselves held up by a problem at customs. At one point the man was in danger of being deported, but with the help of the local MP and the Home Office I managed to get him released and back to Bradford.

I was recently coming home after a stay in hospital. As I walked along a very long corridor on the way out of the hospital with my wife, I met a number of West Indian nurses and cleaners who worked there. They spotted me, and within seconds I found myself surrounded by all these ladies, all hugging me. Marie came to my rescue eventually. This is how our relationship is today, and has been right from the very beginning.

On one occasion somebody counted the different nationalities worshipping in our fellowship. They counted eighteen. I think they must have included the Irish and Welsh and various other borderline cases. The Lord blessed us in every way.

12

Guerillas, Ants and Royalty

Just as 1942 had been a turning point in my life, so 1972 proved to be another significant year. Of the many happenings of that year one stands out in my mind, as it proved to be a foundation for what would happen ten years later when I retired. This was a missionary journey.

I do believe that all our doings are guided by God. A Christian always tries to follow where his Master leads or to go where He sends, but occasionally the Lord speaks very forcefully. It may take many years before His promise comes to pass, but happen it will, if we are faithful

In mid-1972 John and Muriel Davis and their family arrived in Bradford for a furlough. John and Muriel had been missionaries in Thailand for many years and worked very hard to further the gospel in that country. The Lord had led them to Sunbridge Road Mission and the Mission to them; in consequence of which the Mission had helped to support the family for some years. We were very interested in the building up of the Bible Training Camp in Phayao, North Thailand. The church had enjoyed seeing slides of the houses and classrooms being built at Phayao and seeing the people we prayed for regularly. Everyone was looking forward to seeing Muriel and John again after a four-year absence.

Soon after we all met up again John dropped his bombshell. He wanted me to go back to Thailand with him in November of that year to preach at a special conference at Phayao. What an undertaking! Would I be allowed to go? Could I afford to go? Why me? But God does not make mistakes and if it was His will all would be well.

Many obstacles were put before us. The missionary society was very wary of a lay person going into a mission station, and my own trustees were not keen for me to go as it meant a long air journey. They still keenly felt the loss of Mr Fred Mitchell in the first Comet disaster, and they did not want to risk my life also. The money was also a slight stumbling block but the Lord moved many hearts; the money was available when we were given permission to go. John set up the meetings with his colleagues in Phayao and I started my Bible study preparations. Just before we left, the Mission gave us a short Valedictory Service to wish us God speed. They gave us a suitcase each, full of three of everything we would need on our month long trip, some spending money and the films to record our journey. Their prayers and blessings were the greatest gift of all. We left Bradford fully covered by the cloak of the Holy Spirit, knowing that He would be with us all the way. Perhaps here I can say how grateful I am to the many, many people who have prayed for me during my lifetime. I have always been conscious that I could not have achieved anything without their loving care. This missionary journey was a case in point. People prayed, the Lord led us and we trusted and followed.

I remember creeping out of our home at 2.00 a.m. on November 21 in order to reach Gatwick in time for our flight. It rained hard all day; it was the day of the Queen's Silver Wedding Celebrations in London, the Capital was extremely busy, but we made Gatwick in time. I was excited at the thought of a long flight, as it was my first experience of flying. I had enjoyed hearing about my wife's journey by Jumbo jet earlier that year on a visit to South Africa to visit our daughter Jennifer, her husband Terry and our two year old granddaughter, Samantha. Now it was my turn. As only half the complement of passengers was on board we had three seats each and could lie down and sleep most of the way. I have flown many times since but have never had such a comfortable journey.

We finally arrived in Singapore and stayed overnight at a luxury hotel, courtesy of the airline, as we had missed our connection to Bangkok. John and I had time for a quick visit to OMF Headquarters before leaving the airport on our flight to Bangkok.

Bangkok – city of Klongs, golden temples and orchids. An impression of heat, strange smells, noise and traffic jams; rush and bustle; people, people, people. What a crowded city, but so colourful. John and I were driven to the OMF Headquarters and stayed overnight. We still had many hours of travel ahead of us. The following morning we crossed Bangkok to the bus station and boarded a bus for Tak. A bus did I say? Well it had seats and wheels but how it travelled the 400 miles to Tak I will never know. Sitting on narrow wooden slat seats, squashed five to a row and no aisle, we rocketed and plunged over unmade roads for eight hours. We did stop for a meal, but I was so tired I found it hard to eat much. I began to think we would never see Tak, which was a half way point to Phayao.

It had been arranged that we would stay over the weekend at the Mission House of the WEC Mission, and that I would preach the Word to the assembled missionaries. John and I had to travel about three hours through the bamboo jungle in order to meet the missionaries at their "Jungle Conference". The meetings were in the open air and the Lord richly blessed the messages on 'The sermon on the Mount'. Praise the Lord we can meet Him anywhere from city street to bamboo jungle. I remember meeting two young women from Lancashire who had only been in Thailand for about two weeks. They were beginning their first tour of duty as WEC Missionaries. They were both so badly bitten by mosquitoes they could hardly walk. One of the girls had unrolled her sleeping bag and found a nest of cats happily sleeping there. Poor girls, they were finding it all such hard work. I just wanted to send them home straight away and spare them the difficulties of jungle living.

I met up with them a month later and was pleased to see that they were nicely healed and settling down into their new lifestyle. God had been good to them and they were prepared to live for Him in this strange, foreign land. They gave me a lovely gift of a brass candlestick which we treasure to this day.

We left Tak and travelled another 500 miles to Phayao. More misery on that awful bus. The dangers of very fast travel on unmade roads, with drivers who felt that they should be the only ones on the road, were very real. However, we finally arrived at our destination, our home for the next three weeks. We did have one or two longish trips out though. One to Chiang Mi, the old capital of Northern Thailand, and one to the Mekong River. We had hoped to cross over to Laos to visit missionaries, but the communist guerrilla fighting was so close and so fierce that we had to be content with just looking across the river.

On this expedition we passed through a few jungle villages. We were travelling in a Land Rover, John Davis, Dr. Toop, a missionary nurse and myself. The nurse wanted to visit a Meo Christian woman who was due to have a baby. I was left in charge of the vehicle as it was impossible to drive to the Meo village. John, the nurse and Dr. Toop set off, leaving me with these instructions: "If you hear shooting or we do not return in an hour drive down that path as fast as you can. You will eventually find a Thai army post." The Thai soldiers would not venture up the trail as far as we had gone for fear of the guerrillas.

I sat in the Land Rover and thought to myself, "I wonder if the Co-op Funeral Service would come out and pick up my body if I was shot?" The Co-op had promised to bury me, free of charge, at that time as I had conducted many so funerals for them during my ten years in Bradford. I wonder if they would have come? (When I returned home I told this story to the undertakers. They seemed quite disappointed that they had not been able to collect me!!)

After a while I spotted some boys playing football in a clearing. I moved the Land Rover nearer in order to watch them. They were playing barefoot, with a ball made of banana leaves. The ball came over towards me and I automatically kicked it back into play. They then crowded around me and pointed to my shoes. They wanted me to remove my shoes and join them in their game. So I did. Mind you, I left my socks on!

I scored a goal, much to the delight of my side, to raucous cheers of "George Best, George Best". How did they know about George Best in Northern Thailand? I diplomatically changed sides and scored a goal for the other side as well. Once again up went the cry "George Best, George Best". At this point fortunately the missionaries returned. They were running, which missionaries don't often do, and I feared the worst. I was bundled into the Land Rover and we roared away into the jungle.

"Any problems?" I wanted to know.

Apparently they had been able to hear the cries of "Best" and "Englishman over here", over a great distance and knowing that guerrilla troops could also hear them they rushed back to rescue me before the Communists arrived. I was very soundly ticked off by all and sundry.

We did not make it back to Phayao that night. When we realised we were not going to get home we had to find food and a night's accommodation. We parked on the edge of a village, out of sight of the road. We were then able to go to an open air food stall and have a meal. John picked food which I could eat and everyone enjoyed their meal. We then found a house to sleep in. The rooms and a toilet area seemed to be underground. As we prepared for sleep I covered my itchy mosquito bites with a liberal dose of cream, then after prayer I settled down and slept for the rest of the short night. We had to leave at first light for danger was imminent. I reached for my toothpaste in the half light, loaded my toothbrush, put the brush in my mouth and grimaced. I had picked up the mosquito cream by mistake. So what had I put on my bites the night before? Yes – toothpaste; but it worked.

We arrived safely back in Phayao about mid-morning, all of us retiring to bed to catch up on some sleep. I was awakened later by John and the doctor anxiously inquiring if I was well. Did I have a tummy upset? No. I was fine but the doctor and John had been quite ill with diarrhoea.

"Don't worry," I said. "I have some tablets from my doctor. They should help you." It became quite a joke amongst the staff that I managed to keep so well whilst seasoned missionaries were affected by the kind of food they had been eating for years.

Food was quite a problem. I was not allowed to eat fresh fruit unless it had been washed in boiled water. I could only drink boiled water or coke from a can with no ice – that was potentially lethal. The hot curries were a bit too much for me and I did not really like rice. I lost quite a lot of weight on that trip. One food I did enjoy was the sweet pork. It was very palatable and helped to get the rice down. A wooden bowl full of boiled rice was rather boring, so the highly-flavoured pieces of pork were welcome until I learned about the pigs. The pigs appeared to run wild around the villages. They were not penned in any way. I asked why they were allowed to roam. Apparently they were the village scavengers and they cleaned up the toilet areas. I went off sweet pork from then on.

John and I went with another missionary to visit a village high in the mountains, near the Burmese border. We all sat around on the Headman's veranda. I just had to sit still and look intelligent as the meaningless conversation went on. Suddenly an elderly, scantily-dressed lady appeared with a kind of teapot and gave each of us a cup of tea, or so I thought. Having been told never to leave anything I was given as it would be impolite, I drank my 'tea' quickly. It was disgusting. The other visitors sipped theirs very slowly as they talked. To my horror along came the lady and refilled my cup. Again I drank it dry. At that point the missionaries stood up and we all left. John and his friends were doubled up with laughter. It had never been known for anyone to drink two cups of that disgusting brew!

Revival is a wonderful thing, something very few Christians experience except when their own heart is revived. In Thailand I was privileged to feel it, to see it and preach in it; 'it' being almost a living thing, tangible as well as spiritual. I can think of no other way to explain this phenomenon. We heard at Phayao that revival had broken out somewhere in the Golden Triangle, the triangle of Thailand between Burma, China and Laos. It is notorious as the drug-growing area of Thailand. A very dangerous place to go.

John Davis, a German missionary, a Thai pastor and myself left Phayao Bible Camp in the Land Rover on the four-hour journey to the village. I forget the name after all these years and it has probably been destroyed by now anyway. Three-quarters of this journey was on jungle tracks. We parked the Land Rover some way from the village near two other parked vehicles.

As we started towards the sound of singing, we were conscious of the presence of God all around us in a most wonderful way. The Church was only a temporary building: a roof, side pillars and benches. There was a small platform at the front for the preacher. There were upward of a thousand people, hill tribespeople of Thailand packed under the roof and around the building.

John was called up to preach when the singing ceased. He spoke for almost one hour from the Word of God. There was a ten-minute break for worshipful singing, then the Thai pastor spoke for about an hour. Again a short break for singing then it was my turn. John came up on the platform and interpreted my message. I could sense that the other preachers could have gone on and on but they disciplined themselves to one hour. I wondered if I should just speak for half an hour, because with interpretation that would make an hour. No, was the reply, preach for at least an hour. Whilst I waited for the singing to end, in order to preach, I heard loud noises from the jungle.

"Just thunder," said John, calmly.

As an ex-artillery man I knew it was not thunder but mortar fire. Nobody moved and the meeting carried on. At the end of my message on the Beatitudes, Matthew 5, John gave an invitation for the people to come forward and dedicate their lives to Jesus Christ. Quite a number came forward and were counselled. I learned later that four of the men were professional murderers in the tribes.

As the meeting came to a close, the Europeans in the congregation had to make a hurried exit as we knew the Communists were very close. We dashed to our Land Rover and drove away very fast. I was surprised to see the women's vehicle being sent off first while our vehicle brought up the rear. The first two cars were soon out of sight. I inquired why the women's car had gone first and I was told that in the event of an ambush the first car in a convoy was always let through. It would be our car that was attacked if there was to be any trouble. As it happened we were lucky, there was no ambush, although we did see a woman laid out on the road, probably feigning injury, a favourite way of setting up a trap. We rushed past the woman at great speed. We did not slow down, let alone stop, even when the back door of our vehicle came open. We endured the banging until we were safe.

Many of the Christian villages were wiped out by the Communists. The Christians made no secret of their faith, proclaiming it by erecting a large cross at the entrance to the village. Would we in Britain be so brave and stand up for our faith in the face of death, I wonder? We can only pray for our brothers and sisters worldwide who are faithful unto death.

The culmination of our visit to Phayao was the Convention

where I was to preach, through an interpreter, to students, missionaries, pastors and ex-students gathered from all over Thailand. It was very exciting watching all the people gathering for the meetings. They came in all sorts of transport and greeted one another with great joy. The brotherhood of Christians is a lovely thing to see and experience "All one in Christ Jesus". I enjoyed the preaching very much. I felt that the Holy Spirit was with me and I pray that the words I preached were to His glory. Just one incident illustrates the 'fun' of preaching in a mission situation. During one session I glanced down at my Bible only to see a column of ants marching over it. They had climbed up one side of the lectern, were going over my Bible and down the other side. Should I move away? Should I slam my Bible shut? I decided to stand firm and carry on preaching. Good advice at any time to any preacher.

When the Convention ended, John and I left Phayao by bus and went back to Bangkok. After an overnight stay there, we caught our flight back to London and home. We were weary and tired but triumphant and full of praise for our loving Lord who had looked after us so well.

One very special happening during our stay in Phayao was a visit to a leper colony, which was on an island. There was a barrier across the road before the bridge to the island. The patients in the hospital and the villages on the island were cared for by Christian staff. Wonderful things were happening there.

Leprosy has long been a scourge in Thailand, made much worse by ignorance and fear of the disease. It is not as readily transmitted as was once believed. It is not passed on by touch either, as Jesus tried to tell us in the gospels. Lepers used to be treated very badly, often being shut away from their families, to die alone in squalor and anguish. The mission hospitals had worked hard for many years to alleviate the problem, but they did not get the support they deserved because of the fear of the populace. During our visit I heard a lovely story about our Queen.

The Queen was on an official visit to Thailand and requested to see the work of the Christian Leper Hospital. Apparently the officials accompanying the Queen expected her to stop at the bridge and view the site from across the river. However, the

Queen had other ideas. She insisted on being taken into the colony, leaving her car and going on a tour of the wards. She talked to the patients, shook hands with people and showed a loving interest in all the work. The Thai officials were obliged to follow Her Majesty on her tour.

I was told this story by delighted doctors at the hospital, for it had exciting repercussions. The fear of leprosy was going, officialdom was insisting on helping all leprosy sufferers, and when we returned to Thailand in 1983 there was a much better attitude towards the whole problem.

I was so touched by Her Majesty's visit that I wrote and told her how thrilled everybody had been by her visit. I had a very gracious reply from the Palace.

During my visit I had the privilege of preaching in the beautiful little church in the colony. It was a joyous time and one I will never forget.

13
Retirement—a New Venture

As we have already seen I had very many blessings at the Mission and had a wonderful ministry there; but one of the things we had to talk about was at what point I should retire; the normal retirement age being 65. One morning when I was praying in my study I found that the Lord was saying to me that He wanted me to lay down my ministry at the Mission when I became 65. There was no doubt about it, the Lord had made it quite clear to me that I was to retire as soon as I reached the age of 65. I wasn't given any more knowledge than that but I knew that this was one of the times when the Lord had something planned for me to do in the future. I shared this with the brethren. Of course I was only 63 or 64 at that time. Nevertheless, they were very kind about this and suggested that I could carry on until I was 70, as I was fairly fit. I didn't say anything more and just let time go on. Then again a year or so later I had the same experience of the Lord telling me what I should do. This time the message was even stronger and I knew when I got up from my knees that there was no way that I could carry on at the Mission after I was 65. I had no contact with anyone about my retirement apart from the OMF, and at one point Rev. Nick Carr asked me to candidate for the mission field. Although I still had no idea what I was to do I didn't feel that the mission field was the right place for me. I don't think I could have done it anyway.

The time came, and the Trustees gathered together in the study knowing that I was determined to retire. Only then did they arrange to interview a young pastor for the position. The arrangement was made that he would come and join us when I was 65. However the new pastor made it clear that he wanted to come earlier than was arranged. He did not want to wait so long before taking up his appointment. The trustees considered this request and tried to find a way round this problem. In the end they very kindly asked me if I would like to take a year's sabbatical. I didn't really have time to think about it or pray about it but I realised that this was the Lord's way of telling me that this was how things should be. I agreed to do as they wished.

The following Sunday I was in Leeds at a Chinese meeting in the afternoon. I often attended these meetings of the Chinese Fellowship in and around Yorkshire and Lancashire. After the meeting, three young men came forward and said that they had been praying for three years for the Lord to send someone to Singapore to work with the postgraduate students. When these students got home they were having great problems, especially if their families were not Christians. I looked at them in amazement. They saw the look on my face and asked me what I was thinking. I said that I had a free year and I could go. If I had not agreed to take a sabbatical I would not have been able to go. How wonderful that once again the Lord had pointed the way forward for me.

I was soon able to start to make arrangements to leave for Singapore. Even more wonderful was the way the trip developed into a round-the-world experience!

The day of leaving the Mission arrived. The Mission put on a thanksgiving service rather than a farewell service, because after my sabbatical I was to be Pastor Emeritus, a position I hold to this day.

The service was a wonderful experience; people came from all over, many testifying to what the Lord had done for them. It was a very moving service. I have it on tape and it is a wonderful thing to listen to it now and hear how my ministry has helped so many people. The new pastor was to take over from me at the Midnight service on New Year's Eve, 1981. My sabbatical was to start on the first day of the New Year 1982.

I have preached at the mission many times since, but if I am free I like to pop in at the back to see what is going on. It is lovely to meet old friends again. The saddest part of leaving the Mission was leaving my congregation, but as I say they are not mine they are the Lord's. I was only their shepherd and I had the privilege of feeding them. Now someone else is ministering to them, but they are still the Lord's flock.

At last the great day had arrived. It was February 9, 1982, and we were about to embark on a world trip that was to prove memorable. The Mission had planned a farewell service in the morning for anyone who was able to come. The new pastor read from the scriptures, pointing out Paul's journeys. We then had a time of prayer with our son and set off to go to the interchange en route for London, where more people were to meet us to speed us on our way. We eventually arrived at Heathrow where we were to board the plane for Singapore. We had quite a comfortable journey and eventually reached Singapore many hours later.

When we arrived at the wonderful new airport we found that there was a long passage going towards the arrival lounge. Off on the right was the place where we could pick up our luggage. I sent Marie on in front while I got the cases. I told her to look for two Chinese boys who would be waiting for us. She gave me a funny look and remarked that everyone would be Chinese here. I hadn't thought about that. However they eventually found us and took us to our hotel where a meal had been prepared for us. We had already eaten quite a bit on the plane coming over but we sat down and managed to eat something. The hotel was air-conditioned which pleased me greatly. Personally, I find Singapore has a difficult climate, perhaps the most difficult of all the countries I have been to. It is a kind of "bathroom experience" really, all steamy and hot. Nevertheless, we were fortunate to be there. Then Peter Wong, who had founded the Chinese work in Bradford, came to meet us. He whisked us off to another hotel, quite a well-known one in Singapore. Again there was a rich spread of food; we really felt that we must eat at least some of it, even though we really were too full already. The outcome of that over-eating was that we did not feel very well the next day. The Conference we were to attend was to be held on an island off Singapore. Normally we would have gone over on the monorail, but there had been an accident and it was not operating. We had to travel by ferry. When we got to this lovely island, the part of Singapore where the British had their battery guns during the war, we went to one of the old barracks and were given a room. Well, I wouldn't say it was a room, just a single little barrack where four people might live. Our room, unfortunately, had no air conditioning and therefore it wasn't very comfortable. We were introduced to mosquitoes and cockroaches and all manner of other things. However the conference went off very well. The Lord in His wonderful way had brought Mr. and Mrs. Keighley to us. They had been out to Hong Kong, called in at Singapore on their way home, and came to the conference. I suggested that we share the ministry. That plan worked very well. We were allowed just a short time off in an afternoon to go and swim in the lagoon, which was very pleasant indeed. The conference went on all day, and we met so many people that the Lord had put across our paths while we were in that country.

I just want to mention one of them, a lady called Florence. I remember her so clearly coming into my study some years before, having not long been at the University in Bradford starting her academic career. She really was terribly homesick. She cried and I comforted her, saying to her that I would act as her father while she was here. I would help her with anything she needed; all she had to do was to come and ask me. She came quite often and I was able to help her. After Bradford she had to go to a university in Scotland, and I did not see her again. When I met her in Singapore, I asked her if she had succeeded; she replied that she had. When I asked her what she was doing, she told me that she had decided to go into banking. She asked Marie and I to go to visit her and have a real Chinese meal with her. We arranged to go the following day and were given instructions how to get to her bank. We arrived at the bank and looked along the row of people who were working behind the counter. She wasn't there.

We sat down and waited; then someone came and asked who we were waiting for. We told him that we were waiting for Florence and we showed him her card. Immediately we became VIPs. We were ushered into the lift and up to the top of the skyscraper, into the office area where all the senior management had their offices. We were very surprised when we were taken to the Assistant Manager's Office, and when the door was opened, there behind the desk sat Florence. I always remember being very surprised that she had been able to take on such terrific responsibility because I remembered her in Bradford so long ago as a very homesick, unhappy girl. Then a very wonderful thing happened. She picked up the telephone and called a great number of people in high office to let them know I was there. I found that a great number of them knew me because I had led many of them to the Lord. We were taken on a tour of the interesting sites of Singapore and then went to the Headquarters of the OMF. I had been there before on my way to Thailand with the Davises. We were well received there and helped them in the orientation course with some of the young missionaries, especially with one couple whom I had interviewed in the first stages in Bradford. They had gone through all the stages of preparation and were now coming over for the orientation course. It was lovely to see them at the end of their preparation. Normally we only see them off from their home town, but now we had seen them arrive at their final destination. We were able to look after the children while their parents took the course. Marie spent time in the library reading up about Fred Mitchell. It was from that office he was returning home when unfortunately his plane blew up. We found a lot of details that were very interesting.

Our visit there came to an end and we boarded the plane for Thailand.

We landed at Bangkok and as we looked down on to the runway ahead we could see what looked like a zebra crossing. We found out later that it was a kind of crossing, because the Thai people played golf on the airport approach.

Marie had her first taste of Thailand: the terrible smells and the soldiers in the streets with their guns. We arrived at the Headquarters in Bangkok and were very well received. We weren't there very long before we had to set off on our journey to the North. I was very apprehensive about this trip because I had taken this route on my previous visit to Thailand. The buses were very small. Of course they were built for small people, and the seats were just benches. When you got in you sat on one side of the bus or the other, but when the bus was full they pulled a lever and up came seats in the gangway. So once you were in you couldn't move, and the less we say about the speed at which they travelled the better. I was very concerned that Marie would have to travel all day in this fashion. When we got to the bus station with John and Muriel, who were to travel part of the way with us, I found that somehow the Lord had taken a hand in this journey. The buses were modern ones with young Thai girls serving soft drinks. There was even a television above the driver's seat, although it was rather difficult to watch it on the journey.

This was a completely different experience. John had told me that the dangerous mountain roads had been resurfaced (or surfaced for the first time). I thought that would be great, because when I had gone that way before, the roads had been little more than tracks. I didn't really think it was much better: because of the better roads the bus could travel even faster, and there was more than one occasion when we wondered if it would stay upright. Nevertheless we got to our destination and were standing waiting for a bus or lorry to take us to the Bible College. There were a lot of youths about, who got rather excited because they didn't see many white people in that part of the country. I took my hat off and when they saw my white hair they were rather more polite to us. Eventually we were picked up and taken to the Bible School. I had met most of the staff when I was there before. John and Muriel were to join us later.

I had the great honour of teaching the students. John would give lectures in the morning and I would follow in the afternoon, speaking through an interpreter. The Lord led me to speak on the disappointments of the ministry. These young people were in the final stages of their study. Soon they would go out into the villages and wilds of Northern Thailand and preach, set up churches or become pastors of churches that were already there. I told them that the Lord had warned us that some of the seed would fall on good ground, some of it would be snatched away from us and some of it would fall on stony ground. Things would look good and they would think they had a convert, but suddenly they are gone. In Thailand, Christians paid a price by being separated from their friends and family. They would be alright for a time, and then the pressures would get to them and swallow them up, just as they do in this country. We found that the seed did fall on some good ground. Many people were converted, but even among the converts there was a percentage of those who fell by the wayside. But there were always those who gave themselves wholly to the

Lord.

I went on to give a series of lectures from the parables and other things, among them 'Be prepared for disappointment'. Then I spoke at the Conference itself. I got a little bit excited and thumped the Bible as I sometimes do. To the amazement of the students my interpreter, who was a very straightforward unemotional gentleman, a lovely man of God, hit the Bible as well. How they all laughed! Of course I didn't know why at the time, because I was concentrating upon the interpretation. I had already worked with the faculty there. They had come over to study in England to learn English, attending one of the missionary colleges before coming to work with me. Some stayed in our home and so I knew them, especially the principal. Because of my contributions I was given a degree. They told me that it was because they had used my material on the Doctrines of the Church at the layman's level. This had apparently been translated into Thai and had been very helpful to them. They said I deserved my degree. That was a very exciting experience.

We had an experience of another kind. When Marie was going out to Thailand it was suggested to her that she shouldn't take many dresses, because cotton dresses in that part of the world are much cheaper than at home. In Singapore we couldn't get anything that was suitable, but when we got to Thailand, Mrs Davis took her out and they managed to buy some dresses; however, they weren't very good. Marie was so embarrassed when one of her 'dresses' turned out to be a nightdress. That was nothing to the experience she had when we decided to go shopping in the local village. When we got to the village the men were over the moon when they saw Marie, just as some people here would be when they saw a beautiful actress. They wanted to stroke her hands and her arms. Poor Marie, she was so full of fear, but eventually we managed to get her through the crowd. This time she was able to buy a very beautiful Thai dress. Then we had the job of running the gauntlet to get her out again back to the camp. She didn't move out of the camp again after that. Then someone was murdered. I heard the gunfire and automatically rolled out of bed to see what was happening. We were in the upper part of the house. I looked at Marie, who was fast asleep, having taken a tablet to try to get some sleep because she was so weary. I left her there because it was the safest place to be. I went down the stairs to see what was happening to the students below. I was just in time to see a Land Rover driving away into the village. One of the head men in the village was what I suppose we would call a gangster. He had been defrauding the son of one of the leading bandits in the area. The bandit had paid the soldiers to come and shoot him. He was laid out there in the morning and there were all sorts of things going on: wailing, crying and sad music for days. It was very distracting but we watched the funeral go by. That was one of the things we had never seen before.

Once again our stay came to an end and we returned to Bangkok. The people there were very gracious to us. They gave us a holiday before we set off for Hong Kong, and gave us the use of a house on the coast where the missionaries go to rest. There were beautiful sands, though the sea was full of jellyfish; one of the missionaries who was there, an Australian, taught me how to surf. I enjoyed that very much. It was very, very hot and there were lots of lizards. One fell on Marie; she screamed, the lizard left its tail behind and ran off! The only cool place was the library, so you know where Marie spent most of her time. I just wandered round the town. I love to see different places. When we left the holiday home we were able to leave some money for them, to repay their kindness. This would be given to the children of the missionaries to pay for rides and ice-cream; these were the only things that had to be paid for when the missionaries went on holiday at that house. Then we had a very dangerous ride back to Bangkok, but the Lord was with us, our angel went before us and we arrived safely.

Our next port of call was Hong Kong. When we arrived we were met again by many of the Chinese who knew us. They had arranged a special dinner for us in a posh hotel; we sat there and experienced the high life of that wealthy part of Hong Kong. It was Easter, and on the Sunday we went to a special service in the Baptist church on the mainland of Hong Kong. We were staying at a hospital run by two ladies, who used to go round all the rubbish heaps of Hong Kong collecting all the babies who had been thrown out with the rubbish because they were deformed. These unfortunate infants were brought to the hospital and cared for by these wonderful women. There was a small boy there called Daniel who had no arms or legs. At this time Marie had arms and legs covered with bites but she gave thanks for her limbs when she saw Daniel. In the evening we had fellowship with some of the wives of the soldiers who were stationed in that part of Hong Kong. It was very near the border and we could walk up the road and look over into China. They took us up the mountain sightseeing and we had a little service of our own in the evening. Then we were given the use of a flat in which to stay while we were in Hong Kong. It was a very expensive property, which belonged to the parents of one of the men we knew. They were away and he allowed us to stay there.

While we were in Hong Kong we had a very busy schedule. The Monday we arrived it was arranged for me to speak at St Andrew's Church, and I had also been asked to attend a Chinese wedding.

The following day we were to have a day off to look around Hong Kong. After that I was to go to try to help one of the brethren in any way that I could with some of his problems, after which we were invited to a meal at the Diamond Restaurant. Then I was to share ministry at the Faith Baptist Church. On the Friday we again had time for prayer at various services.

On Saturday we visited one of the islands. We went out to the borderland to look across to China and then had a meeting in the flat where we were staying. In the evening we were to help with a group of Chinese who gathered together regularly for meetings, after which I was to visit the man in charge of the work and join in with their fellowship.

Then we had a day for shopping.

I was to speak at the Bradford fellowship meeting; the subject was "God's sovereignty in our lives". Later I was to speak to another group who welcomed us into their home.

The following day we had an outing.

I preached on the 10th in a Baptist church from 3 o'clock to 6 o'clock, and then went to share ministry with the Manchester group of Chinese which also met in Hong Kong.

On the Tuesday we had an informal evening when we had a

great time of fellowship. Friday was a rest day with a meeting in the evening. The following day I had to preach at a seminar for around one hour or so on the scriptures. My subject was "Victorious Christians living in such a competitive world".

On the Wednesday we had a day off to take a trip to various places around Hong Kong.

We then had a day of fellowship with a friend at her home. People gathered there and we were able to minister to them. Then on the Friday we ministered to two different groups of people.

On Saturday we had fellowship in the Faith Baptist Church and I was able to share the scriptures with them.

The fourth Monday I preached at the service in the church with an interpreter. Then we visited a very old part of Hong Kong which was very much like it used to be.

On the Tuesday I had the thrill of being able to visit mainland China. It was a wonderful experience going round the local area of China just over the border. I went alone because Marie didn't want to go.

We went to St Stephen's Baptist church on the Sunday and I preached on "The Second Coming of the Lord". This is a very popular subject in Asia because they are always looking earnestly for His coming again. Then we went to a monthly meeting that they had gathered together. I had the privilege of preaching to them.

Then again at the weekend we had a trip around. There were so many interesting things to see there.

It sounds as though the schedule was very heavy, and it was, but the second time I went to Hong Kong it was almost doubled. It is remarkable the way that the Lord opened up such a wide ministry in such a short time.

There was a young lady who knew me in Bradford and, knowing of my ministry to the dying, she asked if I would help to set up a ministry in their hospital. The Lord was good to us and we were able to do this for them. They wanted to put aside a special wing for those who were dying from terminal diseases. I went with them; we had a great time, sharing lots of things together. A few months after I got home I received a letter to let me know that the unit had been set up and was doing very well.

On our last Sunday we had to get up early because we were going right across Hong Kong, by ferry to Kowloon and then right up into the city centre. The instructions we had been given were not very clear; we arrived rather late to find that everyone had been waiting for us.

When the service started they called upon Marie to give a testimony. There were two interpreters because there were two dialects of Chinese going on at the same time; but she did very well despite the difficulty. Then there was another shock to come. When they gave the notices I heard that I was to preach in a new church that was to be opened in the afternoon. My guide apologised and said that he had no idea that this was going to happen. There was nothing I could do about it, not that I wanted to. We had already planned to have a farewell party in the flat. So everybody else went back to the flat. I had to go off on my own in a taxi to one of the many islands around Hong Kong.

When I arrived there I found that the church was right in the centre of a large block of flats that had just been completed. The purpose of buying that complete area in the middle was to establish the church. They were preparing themselves for the time when Hong Kong would be taken over by China. The church would be hidden in among the flats, among people who would worship there; they would be protected from persecution.

There was a speaker appointed to address the meeting. When I found that he could speak a little English I told him that I didn't think I was to speak, but he told me that I was. I didn't want to take his place but he insisted that we could both speak. We went into the flats and I was given a pair of scissors to cut the white ribbon that signified the opening of the church. There was a short service of dedication. I said a prayer and a blessing for them in this new venture. After a meal I was taken back to Kowloon station. I found my way back to Hong Kong and back to North Point. By the time I got back to the flat the celebrations were almost over.

As you have seen we had a marvellous time right up to the very last moment. We had the privilege of ministering to our brothers and sisters there.

Marie and I loved Hong Kong. I would like to use this

opportunity to thank all those who gave us hospitality and gifts that enabled us to continue on our journey.

14

A Well-Earned Rest

After leaving Hong Kong our next port of call was Japan. We arrived at the airport in the late evening and, although we were the first to leave the plane, we ended up in the wrong queue and were the last to leave the airport. We had to take a very expensive bus journey to the terminal in Tokyo. We were met by one of the OMF missionaries, who took us to the home of another young man who had been on the mission field for a long time. The Lord had used him very well in taking His message from the Gospels to the children in Japan; his work in that field had been very successful.

Later I had the privilege of helping a missionary who was in need. Missionaries can also go through times of depression and problems and this was one of the reasons I felt I had been sent there.

I had the very exciting experience of preaching in a Japanese church and I felt that the Lord blessed that service. The congregation presented us with a Japanese instrument of which we are very proud.

A sightseeing trip around Tokyo had been arranged for us. We were accompanied by a young lady who could speak English to help us with the language problem. We had to stand up all the way on the train or, more correctly, hang on to the handrail. When we got to Tokyo she asked us where we wanted to go. First we said that we would have to get some money. That took some doing but eventually we managed to get some. We then asked if there was a MacDonalds. She looked at us in amazement and told us there certainly was, but it was quite a distance away in the underground city. This was a kind of shopping precinct under the town and we could get to it via the railway station. We hadn't eaten European food since we left home, so that was where we chose to go. Unfortunately that was all that we were able to see because it took us such a long time to get to MacDonalds and then enjoy the meal that by the time we got back to the station it was time to go back home.

We then ventured down to the south of Japan where a missionary, Freda Stanley, had been working for many years with the Japanese Mission Band. When we arrived there it was the time when the blossom was out. The perfume coming from it was wonderful. Freda had a lovely Japanese house shared with a young lady who helped her in the work and we had many exciting experiences there. One strange experience was having a bath. They certainly have a very odd way of bathing in Japan. They do not have normal baths. The water gets very hot and water comes up to your chest. When the first person has finished the next one gets in. Later in our journey we took baths at an inn where the bath was a very large communal one. I was lucky because I took my bath late at night when no one else was there, but Marie and the missionary had great fun when they took their bath. They sat on the plastic ladles that should have been used to pour water over them; the stools slipped and away they went. There were great shouts of laughter.

We enjoyed being taken around to see the churches with which Freda worked. We were very well received and had many great conversations with the people, finding this a very interesting experience. We saw quite a lot of that area where she lived.

We took a flight to Hokkaido, the north island. While we were there we stayed with Fred Mitchell's son who had been out there for many years with his wife. They had a little flat where we stayed, with a large stove in the centre, as it was very cold in the north of the country. They also took us around and showed us various things. He also explained that if anything in a Japanese home is not up to standard or is broken, it is not repaired but put outside the house to be collected as rubbish. The missionaries watch out for this because often the things discarded by the Japanese were far better than anything they could afford to buy. The missionaries' homes looked great. The Lord provides in mysterious ways.

Marie and I were lucky to be able to go to the Bible School

where I spoke to the students through an interpreter. They asked us to join them for a meal. This was something we had never had before—seaweed. I can't say that we enjoyed it but we enjoyed something more than good food. At one point during the lunch one of the missionaries asked the students to greet us in our own language. One by one they stood up and gave us a greeting in English. You could see them practising while they waited for their turn to speak. I thought how wonderful it was that they could do this. As far as I know there would not be many English Bible colleges where, if the Japanese paid a visit, the same thing could be done. That really impressed us. Then they had a special meeting which was preceded by a tour of the area with a loudspeaker inviting people to attend. I had the privilege of preaching at this meeting, once again through an interpreter. They don't get many people to these meetings but it was wonderful to see the dedication of the Lord's people there. On that occasion a young man came forward looking for salvation. One missionary told me that they had worked for many years and never had a convert. That young man is still going on and so is his family.

We went further up the island to another group of missionaries who were working in a very large church. The Lord was pouring out His blessing almost to the level of revival. That was very exciting to see, but again we found the reason the Lord had sent us out in this way. The missionaries here were hungry, not for food, but for knowledge. In Bangkok I had had the privilege of preaching to missionaries who wanted me to speak for two hours on the Second Coming, but at this meeting in Hokkaido the questions that needed to be answered took much longer than that. After coffee, the missionaries gathered round, asking questions and sharing with me all manner of things. They wanted to know so much; it was so exciting to see the hunger for knowledge. The Holy Spirit was so good to me. I was helped to answer all the questions I was asked. The meeting went on and on for hours. I could hardly speak at the end of it.

When we were setting off to go back south, the missionaries walked to the station with us just to give them time to ask a few more questions. When we sat down in the train we were exhausted but very excited. The train would take us to one of the schools for missionary children: this was the school where the Mitchells sent their children. Mrs Mitchell had been almost crying when she stood on the platform with us because it reminded her of the time she sent her children away to this same school.

We suddenly stopped with a jerk, just outside a station, about halfway through our journey. We didn't think anything about it but there seemed to be an awful lot of conversation going on in Japanese which, of course, we couldn't understand. One of the Japanese railwaymen told us in the best way he could, by mime, that there was nothing to worry about. The train was going to be late and we had been told that if a Japanese train was late you could claim money back; so we discussed this while we were waiting. Then eventually we got going, and as we passed at the station we could see a scene of devastation. There had been an earthquake. Earthquakes automatically stop the trains. The jerk we had felt had been the tremor.

The train then travelled very slowly and carefully to its destination. The missionaries who had come to meet us had gone back to the school when they heard that the train would be late. They had left a message to say that they would be back in time to get us to safety before the next earthquake, which would be sure to follow the first. The missionaries eventually arrived to take us to the school and they asked if we had been able to get in touch with home. They had already let their families know they were safe because it was known that they were in the earthquake belt. They allowed us to ring home and I spoke to our son David. They were all so pleased to hear that we were safe because they had seen scenes of devastation on the TV. How wonderful it is that we are able to communicate so quickly from one side of the world to the other.

After a short stay at the school we were to travel towards Tokyo, but had to wait for the level of the sea to subside before the ships could set sail. Apparently the earthquake had disturbed the seabed. We were able to start our journey at last and travelled towards Tokyo. This was a fast train but nothing like the bullet train on which we had travelled before. We were to take three days on this journey, stopping each afternoon at a different station. At each stop there was a missionary waiting to greet us and to take us to where we would stay the night. We had very good fellowship in many homes during that journey. It would take far too long to tell you about all of the homes we visited, but they were many and the people were very friendly. We were very well blessed on that long journey. At last we reached Tokyo and went to the airport. Eventually, weary but full of the joy of the Lord, we set off for Australia.

We had been looking forward to our visit to Australia. The original idea of going there was to meet up with Marie's brother who had gone to live there with his wife many years before. They now had two children, whom we had not seen, and we were to have a holiday and a time of rest with them.

They had a swimming pool, although it was not in use because the temperature was only 70 degrees which, to them, was winter. We enjoyed our time with them and had many opportunities to talk about the Lord. We hoped that our visit to them would be a blessing. It proved to be so because, when I went back on my own on my next trip, I was so wonderfully received. We talked very deeply about such things as salvation of the Lord and the Bible. All too soon the holiday ended and we went on with our travels.

We moved down to a place called Singleton, about 50 miles from Newcastle. I was going to preach in a Baptist church in that area. The minister there was a wonderful man. His comment when anyone presented him with their problems was always "No problem. No problem". We shared a ministry with him and enjoyed preaching at his church and also at three others.

I went back again to that place on my second trip but the minister had moved away; however he invited me to preach at his new churches in the outback. I preached at one church early in the morning and then we moved on to the next church about five miles away; then on again to another church, eventually coming back to the main church for the evening service where I was to preach again. The Lord blessed that evening service in a very strange and wonderful way. After preaching the Word of God and issuing a challenge about our spiritual condition in the sight of God, two young people came to the front of the church. I didn't know them but I could see that the pastor was looking anxious.

They asked him if he would allow them to share with the congregation a problem that they had about which he already knew. He agreed.

They were the church youth leaders. They had fallen into temptation and were to have a child. Although they had planned a wedding for a short time later, they felt that they wanted the congregation to know about this and to ask for their forgiveness. After they finished speaking there was a silence which seemed to go on for ever. Then a member of the congregation slowly came forward and kissed the young couple; followed by the rest of the congregation one by one, until in the end everyone was hugging each other and some were in tears. We then had a time of prayer when we thanked the Lord for the power that He has over us to allow us to confess our sins in the presence of the church and to let us know that we can be forgiven. The church grew in unity from that day.

The following day we went back to Singleton, which was a whole day's journey away. The pastor took us halfway where I was met by another young American pastor whom I did not know. It was a whole day's constant driving. We had only time to stop for a short meal. It was important that we got to Singleton before dark, as it is unwise to travel at night in the outback because kangaroos have been known to jump out and cause accidents. We arrived late in the evening in Singleton. The young man had taken over the pastorate and he and his wife had done such great work. His church had doubled in numbers and these people were so blessed and hungry for the Word of God. I had a great time ministering to them. Then I was asked to visit another church, well into the outback.

I had been invited there to preach for a week. I was to stay with the pastor in his bungalow by the side of the church. The morning and evening services were almost at revival standard. There was a real movement of the Spirit. After the evening service the pastor approached me and told me that there was a young couple who wanted me to go to their home with them. They promised to bring me back for the evening service the following day. One of them was a teacher and the other worked on the land. We travelled for about 150 miles before we arrived at their home, and though it was very late, we had a time of blessing around the Word of God. The next day when we got up they had their Bible open and a list of questions which they wanted me to answer. We sat down throughout the day, only pausing to have food and to stretch our legs. They were so hungry for God's Word. Living in the outback they did not have much contact with people except for a small group who lived near them. They did not know the hymn "Amazing Grace", but they knew the Lord. They had been converted about twelve months before.

We arrived back for the evening service, and again the pastor told me that there was another couple who wanted me to stay at their farm. This time, the farmer had invited all the people who lived in the area to come and have a meeting at his house. Once again they were hungry for the Word of God. Then back to the church where I was asked to visit yet another home. This happened every night and I worked out that I had travelled 800 miles in that week. Distance to them is nothing, but I was feeling very very tired, having preached and talked throughout the whole day, every day. But that, of course, was why I was there. That is what the Lord wanted me to do. That was why I had been called to leave Sunbridge Road at 65. This was what I was called to do. I had been given the opportunity of ministering to those dear people.

I was taken back to Newcastle where I got a train down to Sydney. There I had the privilege of meeting a man who had been a member of our church. He had strayed away from the Lord, but now we just sat and talked with him and his daughter. It came so natural, and I felt very near the Lord while I was in that home.

After all the travelling, at last came the opportunity to have a day off. The Lord put me by the sea and put a rod in my hand, so I began to fish. There was an old gentleman sitting near me. I watched him bring out twenty fish while I only brought out one. It shows that the Lord can use us as fishers of men when we cannot catch the swimming fish. When I got back home there was great excitement because a shark had been seen in the waters near where I had been fishing. I didn't see him and he didn't see me, and so we had no involvement with each other.

Honolulu here we come. It was a long flight from Australia to

Hawaii. It was supposed to be a paradise but Marie did not think so—particularly when she put the lights on after dark and saw the room filled with very large cockroaches. We enjoyed seeing the active volcano there but the purpose of our visit was to see a young lady who belonged to our Church. She had been converted during our ministry and had gone out to work with Waiwan. She had married an American and they worked with the children. We were well received in Waiwan and were invited to attend the prayer meetings; the director invited us to lunch. As we came away from there we were able to help a member of the staff. He did not have any money and he needed to go to Honolulu. We were able to help raise the fare for him. We had already seen poverty among many of the missionaries we had met. The young lady whom we were visiting had not had a new dress for a long time and we were able to help her. We were able, in the midst of all the spiritual enjoyment, to help our friends in a practical way. In Honolulu I was able to visit Pearl Harbour.

Then on to the United States, arriving safely in Los Angeles where we were met by a young man who had done a lot of work helping the people of Romania. He was helping out in one of the churches in Los Angeles. We had a great time of fellowship there with him. We then travelled to San Diego and met up with Bob and Betty Finesmith, two wonderful people. Bob was one of the people who helped Sidlow Baxter with his ministry arrangements when he visited that area. Of course Sidlow Baxter visited Sunbridge Road several times and I had had great fellowship with him. He had recommended us to Bob and so we had a contact. Bob had started a list of appointments for me when I arrived there. Over the years this list has increased. On my last trip it had almost doubled, and we had a great time of blessing wherever we met.

Then we flew to Texas. We had been invited to go there by a group of people who were starting a new fellowship near Dallas. Mr. Stanley Banks, another minister who used to come to our church, requested that we go to help them. I felt sure that we were able to help them although our stay was very short. Our next stop was North Carolina; there we also had a great time of blessing working with a young man whom I have mentioned before. He had been called, during one of our church services, to go into full-time ministry and the Lord has blessed that ministry. We then moved up to Philadelphia, met with the OMF and worked with them. One of our tasks was to attend a conference they had arranged in Montroe, in Pennsylvania. While we were there the secretary listened to one of my messages and then invited me to go back to stay and preach for a week. Then we moved up to Buffalo to see one of the young ladies we met in Thailand; she had invited us to go and stay with them for a few days. She had married a minister and I was privileged to preach in his church.

I would now like to share with you details of the last trip I made: to St. Louis, to a district called Eccles Grove. On our first visit we had travelled by car with Bob and Betty Finesmith from San Diego to St. Louis. This place, about fifty miles from St. Louis, was the place where they had been brought up and we were invited to attend their church to hear Bob preaching. At the last moment he was called back to San Diego, and he recommended that I should take his place. They had never heard an Englishman preach, let alone a Welshman. That service was blessed, so much so that I was invited to go back and preach there for a week. On my next visit to America I went to Eccles Grove first. The church had built up in numbers and became so full that people were standing. Every night there was a response to the invitation to come forward. The deacons came in to help with the counselling. When the ministry finished on the Friday night I was due to have a couple of days rest before flying on to San Diego, but they begged me to stay and preach again. They asked me to preach on the Second Coming. On Sunday I preached at the church and on the Monday I preached twice on Israel and the Word. Then I set off to another church where again I experienced great blessing. When I eventually arrived in San Diego I was very weary. Bob was waiting for me at the airport and he said he was glad that the plane was early because I was due to preach that night. In three months of ministry I had only half a day as a tourist. The young pastor from the church in St. Louis has moved to another area and I have been requested to go and preach there. There are five churches in that area, all of which would like me to share with their ministry. I will go back although I couldn't go this year (1990).

We eventually returned home to Bradford after all the pleasures of this lengthy world trip. We flew into Heathrow and from there boarded the plane to bring us back to Yorkshire.

• • • •

You might wonder what I am doing now after all the excitement of a world trip. Well of course I am officially retired. I still preach at various churches. I go to Sunbridge Road once a year. I help out at churches where there is no pastor and I preach at my son-in-law's church.

I was led by the Lord to listen to the many people who have asked me to write down the things that I have done so that they can enjoy them. I have done this with one purpose in mind. That is to share what the Lord Jesus has done for me. If he can do it for me he can do it for anyone.

You will recall that early in this story I was sent to Gibraltar. Now I would like to end by recounting our visit in 1990. Marie asked me to take her there; so we booked a flight and a hotel, and off we went. Of course it was completely different to the days in 1942 when there were only soldiers on the Rock, as all the inhabitants had been evacuated. We did not go into a barrack room but into a lovely hotel, but it was good to be in the place where I had been converted so long ago. We walked about in the rocks. We went to the little Methodist church in the High Street where I went as often as I could when I was off duty.

I determined that I would do as I had done all those years ago. That was to walk up to the top of the Rock to the spyglass area. I managed to do it, but only just. We also had the excitement of seeing St. Michael's Cave, which was where we kept our ammunition during the war. There were stalactites there but we had never seen them during those dark days. Now it has been made into a sort of cathedral and it is illuminated to show all the wonderful colours. Then I wanted to take Marie to show her the place where I was converted. We could go quite a long way up the hill by lift but we had to walk the last bit. Marie was very tired but she made it. When we got to the top we found that the gates were locked. The guns were still there and I managed to point out things through the gate, but I was very disappointed not to be able to go nearer to them.

We decided to go and have a cup of something in the cafe near St. Michael's Cave, which was not very far away. While Marie went to get the drinks, I sat down. Soon a group of soldiers came in and sat near me. They were talking about the guns. I asked them if these were still in action and was told that they were. They asked how I knew about the guns. They went to fetch an officer when I told them that I had been a gunnery instructor there. The officer asked if I would be willing to help them by giving them some information about a gun that they were trying to restore. I said that we had only just come down the hill and that my wife was very tired. The next thing I knew was Marie was being put in a jeep and off we went back to the top of the hill. As we approached the gates, they opened. My Lord wanted me to be there.

Eventually we got to the gun. I was amazed to see the old gun still there. They had worked very hard on it but there were certain things that they didn't know, and I was pleased to help them. This was one of the guns that was in action during the time I was there. Then I wanted to show Marie where I first met the Lord. As we came out of the gates I asked the officer if I could go through the cave. He did not know there was a cave there. It was from inside the cave that the guns were controlled. Through the other side of the cave there was a way out to look over the Mediterranean. There were steps cut out in the rocks by the Spaniards who had tried to invade the rock. The officer fetched a torch and we went into the cave. He was so excited that he insisted on taking my picture sitting on the rock where I had prayed and studied the Bible all those years ago. Then we had to try to get Marie into the cave. It was rather a difficult task, but we managed it; gradually I was able to lead her to the place where I had been converted.

Isn't the Lord wonderful? He has all the universe to care for and he was interested in a silly little old ex-soldier who was dancing in excitement on the top of the Rock of Gibraltar. He opened those gates and He helped me to get through that cave to let us see what we wanted to see!

It is not always the great and mighty things, but sometimes

the small things like that, that show us the great power and personal love and fellowship we have with the Lord. God Bless you all. Amen.

Postscript

by Mabel Walker, Secretary of the Slackside Wesleyan Reformed Church

It was a bright spring-like afternoon in late February of 1991. I was making my weekly visit to the 'Manse' of the Slackside Wesleyan Reform church, where lived the Minister with his wife Joan and two children (now young adults). The Reverend Rowland Graves had suffered a stroke in November 1990 which had left him with impaired speech and some problems with his right side. The church was without its spiritual leader and as I made my way to the manse I was pondering over the future of the church, its minister and his family.

I little knew that the Lord was already moving and planning the way ahead, nor did I know what was waiting for me as I rang the doorbell.

I called out, "Hello, it's only me". This was my usual greeting, so that if Mr Graves should be alone he knew he did not have to answer the door.

When I went into the room it was to find that Mr and Mrs Graves already had a visitor. It was none other than Douglas Evans who had been pastor at Sunbridge Road Mission for many years. I only knew him by name and reputation as an outstanding preacher. I had been privileged to sit under his ministry on several occasions but had never met him at such close quarters. Imagine my surprise then when after being told who I was he told me I was just the person he wanted to see.

I'm afraid I was rather nonplussed at first but all was to be revealed in the ensuing conversation, the outcome of which proved to be the beginning, for me, of a treasured friendship and a wonderful insight into this gracious and humble man of God.

The Reverend Graves and Pastor Evans had worked together for a great number of years on several evangelical committees connected with the free churches of the city of Bradford. Over those years a deep friendship had developed. When Mr Graves was taken ill, Pastor Evans was naturally distressed at the nature of his illness and a desire arose in him to help a fellow colleague in the faith. It was this conviction that led him to visit Mr Graves that February day. The pastor shared with me his desire to help. He told me that the Lord had guided him to make this decision. He had recently returned from a visit to America and he had begun to feel it was time that he stopped his long distance travelling and settled down at home. However he was restless and wondered what work the Lord had for him at home. He had no intention of giving up preaching and spreading 'The Word' he loved so much. He was certain that the Lord had not finished with him yet and that certainty was made clear when he found that there was every possibility that his friend, Rowland Graves, would not be able to preach again. There and then he offered his services to the Slackside Church and, if the church agreed, he would serve for the next three months, when the situation would be reviewed.

It was with a great sense of relief and joy that I was able to take such news to the leaders of the church who readily and gratefully accepted the gracious offer.

From the time that Pastor Evans began his pastoral oversight of the church, he has endeared himself to the hearts of our people, young and old alike. The fellowship has begun to benefit from his wide experience of God's word. Such is his enthusiasm and desire to fulfil his Lord's will and purpose, that, when he was not feeling in the best of health, just after Christmas 1991, he was determined not to fail the church and fulfilled commitments in the New Year, when perhaps he ought to have been resting.

In conversation with him about this time, I was anxious that he should not overtax himself and suggested that I find someone to fill his Sunday appointments in January 1992. He would not hear of it and said quietly, but firmly, "No one, having put his hand to the plough, and looking back is fit for the Kingdom of God." So who was I to make such a man feel unfit for the Kingdom?

My phone rang one day, shortly after this chat, and lifting the receiver, as usual wondering who could be ringing me, a voice said, "Hallelujah, good Evans here." I couldn't help but chuckle at such an unexpected greeting, which was the first of many such greetings. How it lifted my spirits for, unknown to "good Evans", I was feeling a little low that day and the infectiousness of the greeting cheered me immediately. The 'good Evans' was not, of course, a boastful spirit but rather a mischievous one, showing another side of the man's character. This greeting must have cheered many a soul and put many a person at ease and in a happier frame of mind without him ever realising it.

He always consults me and asks my opinion, insisting that I am the 'boss'. When I tell him that it is he who is the boss, again he insists that I have to correct him and show him the way. If you knew my humble beginnings and background you would realise what an amazing thing this is to me. He is very careful to keep his friend, our minister, informed of any of his plans and always seeks his blessing on anything he wishes to do.

When Easter 1992 was on the horizon the Pastor began to make his plans and asked permission to have leaflets printed with details of the special services to be held. Permission being granted, 600 leaflets were printed and ready for delivery to homes in the area around the church. Pastor offered to help deliver the leaflets and when I said that we had enough help he still wanted to do his bit. So typical of this great character. This man, 73 years young, said he never asked anyone to do a task that he was not willing to do himself. However willing, this time it was not to be, other circumstances took over (or was it God's overruling power?). The task was completed by the youth of the church. The Easter weekend proved to be a time of rich blessing and fellowship within the church. We had a new and greater insight brought to us of what Easter is really about.

About this time Pastor Evan's health was giving cause for concern to his dear wife Marie and his family. You will have already read that they are all with him in his work, giving him all the love and support they can. Such was his determination to fulfil all his promises to the church that he still carried on, when at times he should have been resting and taking life a little easier. Eventually a Christian doctor, a close friend, stepped in and endeavoured to make him realise that if he wanted to continue preaching in the future he should have a rest and a change. As you can imagine he found this news a bitter pill to swallow.

One day I was busy with some church work when the phone rang and a voice that I did not immediately recognise said, "Hello, it's Pastor Evans." What, no Hallelujah? I knew straight away that something was amiss. He had rung me to let me know that he was going to see a specialist and he would let me know the result as soon as possible. I waited with some anxiety for a few days for him to contact me. When he did it was his usual cheery "Hallelujah" that he announced that there was nothing serious wrong, it was 'only angina'. After a word with Marie I felt that he really should take a rest and it was arranged for him to be released from his appointments until the end of June, so that he could take life a little slower for a while. But such is his zeal and love of preaching that he does not find it easy to 'sit at ease in Zion' and watch his family all busy in the Lord's service.

We look forward with eager anticipation to his ministry and leadership again. I believe we are already seeing the fruits of his work amongst us. The fellowship at Slackside Church has been greatly encouraged by the knowledge that unknown friends and fellow Christians all over the city of Bradford and beyond have joined in the great fellowship of prayer for the Reverend Graves and his family, and for our church as a whole. We owe so much to all these friends, known and unknown, and most of all to Pastor Evans whom we cannot thank enough for the great love and concern he has shown to us. This would have been a very difficult period in the history of our church had it not been for the tremendous help afforded to us. Nor do, we forget the his wife, Marie, who, like all ministers' and pastors' wives, has worked quietly in the background giving him, and us, her support.

The holiday in the USA that the Pastor and Marie had planned has had to be cancelled, due to more and increased concern about his health. He now needs to go through various tests to find the extent of his trouble, but with his usual optimism, great faith and strength of character he is not going to allow this setback to deter him from his promise and desire to preach and to serve his Lord through his ministry at Slackside.

How do you make such a man of God think seriously about a health problem? As Marie has said, "He takes an aspirin and thinks it disappears." You cannot keep such a person down, one who is absolutely convinced of his calling; and who would really try, if it meant going against God's will and purpose?

I have been delighted to add the postscript to his life story. Until a comparatively short time ago I only knew him by name and reputation, but these last months of working with him have been a privilege. I have come to know more personally the man behind the name. I have come to respect and appreciate his strength of character, his zest for his life work, his knowledge of the Bible, but above all his great and sincere love of his Lord. Through his preaching of the word of God, from friendly conversations and the example of his Christian witness he has imparted this love and knowledge to me and to all who have the privilege of knowing him. He has revealed himself as a man of great integrity and compassion with a deep and earnest desire that all might know the love of God for themselves.

How can I faithfully and truthfully sum up my thoughts about this gracious man of God? I have not known him for very long but now I count him and his wife Marie amongst that precious list of Christian friends, such is his gift of communication with all who meet him on his journeyings. I feel that there is no better way than in turning to the Bible that he loves to read in Micah, Chapter 6, verse 8, "What doth the Lord require of thee but to do justly and to, love mercy and to walk humbly with thy God?"

I feel that I can say without fear of contradiction that Pastor Douglas Evans has fulfilled and will continue to fulfil these requirements. I am sure that when his Lord finally calls him to his eternal rest, when he reaches the gate of heaven, the angels will say "Hallelujah, it's Pastor Evans."